Story BONES

How to X-Ray Any Novel for Plot, Conflict, & Character

Mary Lynn Mercer

First ebook edition, December 2013

First print edition, February 2014
ISBN: 0-615-94367-5
ISBN-13: 978-0-615-94367-1

Cover image of skeleton against black background: Sebastian Kaulitzki / Shutterstock. Cover image of old book: Zaretska Olga / Shutterstock. Image of skeleton against white background: Sebastian Kaulitzki / Shutterstock. All images used under license.

Book cover design by: Mary L. Mercer 2014

"Antonio" font by Vernon Adams. "Avenir" and "Avenir Next Condensed" fonts by Adrian Frutiger. "Gentium Book Basic" by Victor Gaultney. "League Gothic" font by Caroline Hadilaksono & Micah Rich. "Lobster" font by Pablo Impallari. "Simonetta" font by Brownfox. "Vollkorn" font by Friedrich Althausen. All fonts used under license.

About the Author

Mary Lynn Mercer's first nonfiction book, *Story Bones: How to X-Ray Any Novel for Plot, Conflict, and Character,* hit #1 on Amazon's Kindle Screenwriting bestsellers list the first week of release. An experienced national contest judge, avid reader, and movie buff, she enjoys applying creative tools gleaned from years of study and pleasure reading to her own writing. For information on other and future releases, please visit her website at *MaryMercer.weebly.com.*

ALSO BY MARY L. MERCER:

The Midpoint: How to Write the Central Turning Point with Emotion, Tension, & Depth

Story
BONES

For Mom

Table of Contents

Introduction

Have you ever run up against a story problem that made you want to beat your head against a wall, wishing for a way to correctly diagnose and treat it? Is a manuscript lying paralyzed in a desk drawer somewhere, waiting for a broken conflict to be mended? Do you long to line your characters up in front of an X-ray machine so you can peer inside them?

Maybe it's time to call in a consulting team of "specialists," experts in their field who've been there, done that, and have the published novels (and reader fan base) to prove it. Consider your favorite authors as doctors who, for the price of their novels, can be called at any time to provide insights into a difficult case.

Solomon once said, "There is nothing new under the sun." Whether you believe there are seven beats, thirteen motivators, or thirty-six dramatic situations, it's all been done before. And that's very good news. Because it means we can learn what other writers did right, what they might have done better, and how to make our stories uniquely our own. All while satisfying the reader.

Ernest Hemingway is gone, but his Pulitzer prize-winning depiction of *The Old Man and the Sea* is available to anyone yearning for a clue about how to handle a solitary character in a cramped, isolated setting.

Jennifer Crusie's *Bet Me* is a good bet for anyone writing realistic plus-size romantic heroines. And Tolkien's take on mastering an ensemble cast lives on as immortal inspiration in *The Lord of the Rings* trilogy.

Staying up with the latest trends in the market is important and styles change, but creatively speaking, learning has no expiration date. A bestselling novelist from the 1920s worked the same magic with his readers as any bestselling novelist on a grocery store bookrack today. Because writers of all eras and genres have the same bones, flesh, and blood to work with: plot, conflict, and character. From these the best writers succeed in fashioning stories that touch thousands, sometimes even millions, of people for generations.

Three-Act Structure

Plot is a character motivated to take specific action, who through facing conflict in pursuit of a specific goal, changes for better or worse. Those seven elements — character, motivation, action, conflict, goal, theme, change — are like vessels the author fills with their unique interpretation of life. Consider the familiar plot of "boy meets girl and falls in love, then boy loses girl, but eventually boy gets girl." Shakespeare's *Much Ado About Nothing* and *The Taming of the Shrew* are both romances, yet Benedick and Petruchio are as different as any two characters can be, and so are the actions they take in pursuit of their respective lady loves. At their most basic concept, both stories share the same plot, but because the elements are different and create a unique combination, they stand apart and live on through time.

One of the keys to a great plot is appreciating the irony of "The same, but different." The same plot, differently told. Even so, all those elements together will languish as a formless void on the page, unless something provides shape, design, and context. Unless something unites and infuses them with meaning.

Here's where I'm about to use a dirty word. (At least, it may be to some people.) So brace yourself. Be strong.

It's... Structure.

There's no getting around it. Structure is the skeleton that a story hangs on. When a novel is structured well, those bones do their job beneath the surface, unseen, supporting the story. When a novel is structured poorly, it's like a Halloween bodysuit with white bones painted on it. Two-dimensional. Fake.

The difference between "formula" and structure is the difference between Romeo and Juliet kissing at the party because it's a certain page number in the story, then returning to the family feud as they were before (formula), versus Romeo and Juliet kissing at the party and realizing they are seriously attracted to their family's bitter enemy and there is no going back to the way things were before (structure). It's not about the kiss. It's about what it means to the characters. In Romeo and Juliet's case, it means a life-or-death choice between romantic love and family loyalty. Structure presents them with a values-based choice, which by its nature demands meaningful change. That's how structure sifts the dross from a character's values to reveal a golden truth concerning human nature.

Some writers reject the concept of structure out of fear it stifles creativity and mechanically produces cookie-cutter facsimiles of original art. The truth is, structure makes certain that all the story's parts are functioning at optimum performance. Structure is about function. Just as the hand performs a different function than the foot, or the mouth than the ear, so parts of a story serve different purposes in service to the whole. And just like bones, these story parts only make sense when fit together in a certain order. It's flesh (conflict) and blood (character) that makes a skeleton unique and individual, but it's the skeleton that gives shape and design to that mass of flesh and blood.

Structure engages the reader's emotions, because it's what gives a story meaningful movement. That's what stories at their heart are all about. Change that means something significant to the main character, and thus, to the reader. An old fisherman regains his self-respect = change. A boy and girl fall in love, happily ever after = change. An underestimated hobbit heroically saves Middle Earth = change.

And structure is how that change is built into the plot, the conflict, and the characters. It's through understanding a novel's structure that the secrets of plot, conflict, and character are revealed.

At its most basic, a story's structure is divided into three thematically unified Acts. The same Three-Act Structure described by Aristotle in his *Poetics* (c. 335 BC) after sitting through countless Grecian plays. Various cultures and literary disciplines have experimented with four-act and even five-act structures, but most of these experimental concepts either have been abandoned or are merely reinterpretations of the original Three-Act design. For example, a Four-Act structure is proportioned the same as a Three-Act structure whose middle act has been divided in half. Since both structures have a natural midpoint that shifts the action in a new direction, dramatically there is almost no appreciable difference between Three-Act and Four-Act Structure.

The Roman poet Horace (65 BC - 8 BC) and the German playwright-novelist Gustav Freytag (1816 - 1895) both advocated the Five-Act Structure for stories, but neither were able to evoke public affection for it strong enough to rival that held for the Three-Act Structure. Shakespeare's plays were first published in five acts a hundred years after his death, and controversy remains as to whether or not they were originally written in three acts. It took the expansive intrusion of television commercials in the 1990s to coerce the public into accepting five irregularly divided dramatic acts, much to the creative consternation of many a network television writer. Twenty years later, more TV ads forced another artificial division, this time into six dramatic acts. (With the addition of teasers, sometimes it's now seven acts!)

The technological advancements of DVD/Blu-ray box sets, DVR equipment, and online streaming enable the public to avoid commercials and watch television shows uninterrupted. However, many of these shows were crafted around the new Six-Act Structure, and viewed with or without commercials, the psychological response evoked in the audience is the same. Each short act rushes through a lot of story material to set up the next act. Emotional development can be shortchanged. Because it's significantly harder to craft six acts into an engaging story that connects with wide audiences, fewer and fewer scripted shows based on this structure become hits. Television writers on social media sites frequently and passionately argue for the death of the Six-Act structure that is now the industry standard. Only time will tell all the ramifications of society and cultures inculcated with this new dramatic structure. Will it drive audiences to pay-cable offerings, where Three-Act Structure still rules? Will it breathe new life into book sales? One thing is evident already. The new scripted stories on television that are shaping minds and hearts today feel very different from those modeled after the Three-Act Structure that engaged societies the world over for thousands of years.

So what dramatic purpose does each of the acts in a Three-Act Structure accomplish? In other words, what makes each act different from the rest, even while together serving the story as a whole?

Act One comprises the first twenty-five percent of the story and is occupied primarily with developing reader interest and identification. This is where the main characters are established, and their significant goals and conflicts set up. While backstory exposition is restrained to the bare-bone necessities at this point, motivations for present actions are strongly hinted at.

Act Two makes up the middle fifty percent and is the actual meat of the story. This is where the main character encounters increasingly hardcore obstacles to achieving what he wants, and experiences the majority of his character growth. It's also where backstory may be eventually explored.

Act Three fills out the last twenty-five percent of the story. It's about the aftermath or what happens once the main character achieves what he's after or fails to get what he wants. The story isn't over, because now he has to prove he's learned the lessons of the preceding acts and put them into practice toward a new but related goal with even higher stakes than before.

EXAMPLE

The Hound of the Baskervilles, by Sir Arthur Conan Doyle

Act One – Establishes Sherlock Holmes as a brilliant detective and Dr. Watson as his capable associate. Introduces the Baskerville curse, and its newest prospective victim who becomes Sherlock Holmes's client. Also a mysterious and clever stalker makes a mocking appearance. Holmes and Watson's goal is to ascertain if a genuine threat exists against their client.

Act Two – Dr. Watson investigates the nature of the threat against their client, while simultaneously playing bodyguard. Holmes and Watson's goal is to identify who or what is behind the threat to their client's life and keep him safe.

Act Three – Having identified the murderer at the end of Act Two, Holmes and Watson's goal changes to trapping the murderer by using their client as bait.

As evidenced by the above example, all three acts are unified by character and related intentions, but are unique in how they serve the purpose of the story. This is as true of the internal story landscape as the external. The theme of *The Hound of the Baskervilles* has to do with superstition versus logic. Even while Holmes is depicted as the personification of logic, Act One is weighted heavily in favor of superstition as many mysterious events occur. In Act Two, these thematic values struggle for supremacy, with evidence stacking up alternately in each one's favor. In Act Three, logic achieves the upper hand and exposes superstition as a deadly fraud.

The Protagonist

The stories that resonate strongest with readers have main characters with a purpose, a goal, a want. Something that drives them to take measurable actions that shape and define the course of the story. It's hard, if not impossible, to develop interest in someone who drifts aimlessly page after page, no matter how nice they are. Main characters with a purpose mean the actions they take possess intention, and it's through that intention that the fabric of their character is revealed. Misunderstandings or accidents may occasionally get them into trouble, but never get them out of it. They have to work hard for their satisfying ending.

The strict definition of "protagonist" means the leading character, but its practical definition is much broader and profound. The protagonist is the character with the biggest want. He urgently desires something or wants to accomplish something. He's also the one facing the greatest opposition to achieving it.

It doesn't matter if it's Anne of Green Gables, Michael Corleone, or Scarlett O'Hara. A protagonist can be good, bad, or controversial. (Though never indifferent, please!) He or she is the protagonist because it's their desires that define the primary physical, emotional, and spiritual goals in the story.

And if he fails, it means death. Irrecoverable loss and separation on a life-altering scale. It could be physical death, as in Suzanne Collins' dystopian novel *The Hunger Games.* It could be emotional death, as in the romantic movie *An Affair to Remember.* It could be spiritual death, as in Hesba Stretton's *Jessica's First Prayer.* Certainly the stakes in a story can involve all three, but the point is they are focused most strongly on the protagonist. It's Katniss who faces the ultimate stakes in the *Hunger Games*, not Prim or Haymitch or even Peeta. Though he faces the same physical stakes in the Games, her spiritual stakes are greater because of her character arc.

Isolating the character with the greatest arc—the character who changes the most from beginning to end—is a strong indicator in many if not the majority of stories as to the protagonist's identity. But it's not a hundred-percent rule. Think of series protagonists or John Wayne's characters in most of his movies. Those characters seldom change, since they often begin the story with a rock solid foundation of moral principles. In *Rio Bravo* it's the drunken sheriff (Dean Martin) who changes the most as he struggles to overcome heartbreak and despair to clean himself up and help defend the town. Yet John Wayne's character is clearly the protagonist and drives the action.

Another good rule of thumb to go by is to look for the character who makes the key decisions in the story. Most of the time it's the protagonist. Occasionally another character will step in and trigger a major turning point, but even then the focus of that character's act is to prevent or provoke the protagonist's acting.

Sometimes the best indication of the protagonist's identity is at the beginning and near the end. Who shows up first with some kind of trouble? Who fights the last battle for the greatest stakes and makes the biggest sacrifice? It's the protagonist every time. Guaranteed. And if it's not, then something is unbalanced about the rest of the story. Because with everything worthwhile hanging in the balance, and after all he's gone through to get to the end, any protagonist worth his salt will elbow other characters out of the way to participate in the last and grandest battle of all.

Even in ensemble stories, such as J.R.R. Tolkien's *The Lord of the Ring* trilogy, one character will rise above the others at key moments. Though readers spend great amounts of valuable time following major characters like Aragorn and the "little hobbits," Frodo is the chief protagonist. He's the one who volunteers at Rivendell as the Ringbearer. He's the one who breaks up the Fellowship on the borders of Mordor to protect his friends. He's the one who ultimately stands on the edge of Mt. Doom with the fate of Middle Earth literally in his hand.

Antagonists and Villains

It's an old but true adage that the strength of a protagonist ultimately rests with the antagonist. Imagine a giant professional weightlifter rippling with muscles the size of tree trunks. No one's impressed if he shows off by lifting a paperweight off a desk. But watch him pit his strength against a pickup truck that's rolled over on a child, and the crowd holds their breaths in awe.

Quite simply, there would be no James Bond 007 without an arch-enemy bent on world domination.

Of course, antagonists don't necessarily have to be evil. It's only when they're willing to cross moral boundaries and harm others to achieve what they want that antagonists enter a whole different dimension and become villains. Even then, they probably don't think of themselves as evil, just highly motivated. Villains have developed belief systems that allow them to do extremely negative things for (in their minds) positive outcomes. In Dodie Smith's *The Hundred and One Dalmatians* (filmed later as *101 Dalmatians*), Cruella de Vil believes that being pretty and stylish is worth kidnapping and butchering hundreds of Dalmatian puppies for their coats.

Villains at their core are extremely intolerant people who feel compelled to wipe out and annihilate any worldview that challenges or competes with their own. The protagonist is an affront to them, as representing what the villain believes is most wrong about society and the world. The more the villain learns about the protagonist, the more personal his struggle to defeat him becomes. As in Dean Koontz's *The Good Guy*. When the villain learns of the protagonist's heroic backstory, it so offends his worldview that he ignores his handlers' orders and doubles down on his efforts to kill him. Before, the protagonist was in danger of becoming collateral damage. Now he *is* the target.

The dramatic connection between villains/antagonists and protagonists is dynamic and interesting because the contrast between them highlights one another's beliefs, choices, and actions. The villain represents the ultimate manifestation of the protagonist's dark side. The reader doesn't have to guess how bad things will be if the protagonist fails to overcome his flaw and change (or in a John Wayne-style story, ever lose his moral principles). The villain is a walking, talking warning sign.

So what about the type of antagonists who *aren't* scheming to take over the world or skin a bunch of cuddly puppies?

The antagonist still struggles against the protagonist over a goal, and still represents an alternative worldview, but is never out to harm others in order to promote their own wants or beliefs. For example, the antagonist in a romance isn't the heroine's lecherous boss or the hero's lying ex-girlfriend. (Their immoral qualities make them villains.) The antagonist in a romance is the love interest, because it's the love interest who struggles against the protagonist's flaws and pushes him or her to change. The love interest represents on some level who the protagonist needs to become to achieve his or her happy ending. That's why the "opposites attract" theory is so frequently on display in romances. It's not just for the inherent external conflict generated by a waitress falling in love with a literature professor. It's about the opposite value systems playing tug of war for the protagonist's soul. That literature professor will never be truly happy unless he learns the joy of living exemplified by the waitress.

Even without a romantic element in a story, the antagonist's job remains to apply pressure on the protagonist to change his chosen course. For example, in Lauren Brooks's first Heartland book, *Coming Home*, the protagonist's sister returns home following their mother's death and wants to sell off their rescue horses to make ends meet. The protagonist wants to keep things the same and continue her mother's work healing abused and dysfunctional horses. Though the teenage protagonist may feel at times that her sister is heartless, she's not a villain. They struggle over not only the future of the ranch, but over values and lifestyles.

A story may have a hierarchy of antagonists or villains, nevertheless one will rise to the top as the protagonist's primary opposition. Even in a thriller like *Die Hard* with a whole crew of thieves and kidnappers, there's only one Hans Gruber to mastermind the struggle against John McClain. Regardless of whether the story is a romance or a western, it's the chief antagonist/villain whom the protagonist wrestles against during all the key moments and the climactic battle at the end.

Throughlines

Story structure has often been depicted as a flat line, broken up into sections by dots and dashes indicating where certain types of scenes should play out. Often like a diagram of the human anatomy hanging on a doctor's office wall, it's dispiritingly one-dimensional and often uninspiring. Not to mention crowded, with over half a dozen story elements shoehorned in.

Instead, what if story structure was expressed not as a flat line but rather like a skeleton with shape, twists, and movement? And not as a one dimensional drawing, but as a holographic image complete with layers of flexible cartilage and life-giving marrow? What if all those disparate story elements were platformed in four simple throughlines weaving like sinew around each bone and joint, uniting the whole skeleton?

Throughlines differ from subplots, in that subplots thematically support but exist largely separate from the main story, intersecting at a few critical points. Often subplots feature a character other than the main story's protagonist as their lead. Throughlines are what make up the main story, and while not every throughline features the protagonist as the lead, every throughline is about showing another dimension of the protagonist's journey.

The four main throughlines in every story are—

The External Throughline — This follows the protagonist's pursuit of the big external goal in the story, and is the primary throughline in most action-driven genres (mysteries, thrillers, westerns, sci-fi, fantasy, etc.), meaning this throughline generates the most scenes and drives the major turning points. In a mystery, it's the detective's attempts to solve the murder. In a romance, it's the heroine's efforts to save the ranch. In a thriller, it's the hero's trying to stop the terrorists from blowing up the building.

The Internal Throughline — This follows the protagonist's internal character arc, his growth into a better person. (Or worse person, if it's a tragedy.) In a mystery, it might be the detective's progression from a person who trusts no one, to someone willing to rely on others. In a romance, it might be the heroine developing from someone who doesn't fit in, into the person who sticks when the going gets rough. In a thriller, it might be the hero changing from an arrogant jerk into someone who appreciates and supports the strengths of others.

The Antagonist's Throughline — This follows the antagonist and how he connects with the External Throughline. The antagonist opposes the protagonist. If he is also morally evil, then he's a villain. Most stories have one or the other, while some have both. In a mystery, this throughline has all the scenes where the murderer covers his tracks and makes it harder for the detective to unravel the case. In a romance the antagonist is often the love interest, so these could be the scenes where the hero's goal of raising an experimental breed of sheep collide with the heroine's goal of saving her family's cattle ranch. In a thriller, these scenes might include the terrorists cutting off the hero's communications and trapping him on the roof of the building.

The Relationship Throughline — This follows the core relationship at the heart of every great story: that between the protagonist and the love interest. The love interest doesn't necessarily have to be romantic in nature. It could be the heartfelt relationship between a boy and his dog, a father and his son, or two best friends. In a mystery, it might be between the private detective and the career cop handling the case. In a thriller, it might be between the hero and his young son who's been taken hostage by the terrorists. The protagonist and the love interest spar in this throughline about ways of doing things, behaviors, and attitudes. The key is that this relationship, above all others in the story, measures the protagonist's internal health. This relationship starts off shaky, or downright estranged, or maybe nonexistent, but its health and survival depend utterly on the protagonist's growth arc. That's why the love interest is also sometimes called the "stakes character," because she personifies a positive potential outcome for the protagonist. In some significant way, she is what he wishes to become. In romances, this is the primary throughline, generating the most scenes and all major turning points.

Throughlines layer a plot with holographic dimension, making it leap off the pages and into the reader's imagination. To explore the concept of throughlines in depth, I highly recommend Carol Hughes' book, *Deep Story*, which is based on her popular writing workshop by the same name.

Events and Sequences

There are many excellent story structure templates available for in-depth study, explored in how-to books by some fabulous teachers. Blake Snyder's *Save the Cat!* trilogy of books. Christopher Vogler's *The Writer's Journey*. Jeffrey Alan Schechter's *My Story Can Beat Up Your Story!* Michael Hauge's *Writing Screenplays That Sell*. Billy Mernit's *Writing the Romantic Comedy*. Sid Field's *Screenplay: the Foundations of Screenwriting*. Alexandra Sokoloff's ebook *Screenwriting Tricks for Authors*. Kim Hudson's *The Virgin's Promise*, which explores a feminine-centric version of Vogler's Hero's Journey and is commonly referred to as the Heroine's Journey. Most of these books use terms unique to the authors, but agree in principle on certain key factors common to successful story structure.

The structure of a story is made up of **sequences**, each one focused on an **event**. Sequences are a series of scenes unified by a single goal or purpose. They are the bones. Events are single scenes where something significant happens that provides momentum, increases the stakes, and swivels the story in a new direction. They are the joints. When strung together, sequences and events form the complete skeleton of the story, upon which are layered the flesh and blood of conflict and character. Sequences and events give the story shape.

How do you distinguish an event from any other scene in a sequence?

I first recognized the difference while reading a series of mystery novels by the same author. The series followed an amateur sleuthing couple, and in one book they stumbled upon a dead body about halfway through the story. This was a major upset to them, because the victim was their best friend, someone they had been trying to help. It turned the whole story from trying to find out what terrible secret their friend was hiding (so they could help him), to finding his killers (so they could get justice for him). This scene was a major **event**.

In the next book, the same couple stumbled upon another dead body about a third of the way into the story. This time, the victim was a potential witness whom they intended to question regarding an earlier crime. His murder presented an obstacle to the couple, forcing them to go elsewhere for the sought-after information. But it did not change their larger plan or purpose. This scene was part of a **sequence**.

Events, because they are major turning points in the story, always involve the protagonist and often are written in his point of view. Other scenes in sequences, on the other hand, may be spiced with subplots that do not directly involve the protagonist.

Characters have a story goal, which means a goal that spans the length of the story, and they also have sequence goals. These are goals which support the larger story goal, but which span the length of a single sequence. For example, a character in a thriller might have the story goal of stopping a bank heist. His goal, spanning a sequence of scenes, might be to lure some of the robbers into a trap to whittle down their numbers. Smaller scenes making up the sequence may have lesser supporting goals of setting the trap, luring the robbers into it, and springing the trap.

Events, even those that spring a major surprise on the main character and/or reader, are what sequences are ultimately about. All the other scenes in the sequence either build up to or cascade down from the associated event. Thus, events are strategically placed for maximum dramatic power either at the beginning or the end of a sequence.

As in the opening sequence of Act Two in Suzanne Collins' *The Hunger Games.* Early scenes cover the three days of training in the Capitol, when Katniss accustoms herself to new weapons and picks up a shadow, the young girl Rue who reminds her of her sister Prim. More scenes relate Katniss and Peeta privately exhibiting for the Gamekeepers, where she loses her temper and shoots the apple out of a roast pig's mouth. There's a flashback to Katniss and Gale's first meeting in the woods. Then a scene where Peeta's request for separate coaching makes Katniss feel betrayed. More training scenes, this time in preparation for the televised interviews. Another scene with Katniss's less-than-spectacular actual interview.

All of these scenes are about training and preparation in the Capitol. And all of them have been steadily building toward something significant to Katniss's character growth. Something that will challenge her erroneous belief that showing love and tenderness is equivalent with weakness. Something that will place her in a stronger position to win the Games precisely *because* it strips bare an emotional vulnerability that everyone can identify with.

It's the scene of Peeta's televised interview, when he confesses an unrequited love... for Katniss! This is the event that the whole sequence has been building toward. The culmination of all their preparations. It poleaxes her right between the eyes, because suddenly no one's interested in how tough or skilled she is. Everyone's focused on Katniss's ability to respond to love. Something she's never let herself be good at, because tenderness feels so weak. Never mind that Haymitch insists it's part of the Game, it's her fear made real.

Because events are where plot and character intersect more powerfully than other scenes, there is a push-pull dynamic to them. The "pull" comes from new information delivered via the plot's action. Someone reveals something to the main character that he didn't know before. Or the main character discovers something he didn't know before. Either way, the information exerts pressure on him, "pulling" him in a certain new direction. The "push" comes from the character's own goals and motivations, what he wants to achieve and why. These internal energies "push" him to make a new decision, often requiring character growth and a change or adjustment in values, and advancing the story in a different direction. So when Peeta reveals he's in love with Katniss (pulling her in a new direction), her determination to succeed in the Games (push to make a new decision) forces her to grow and change. She's going to have to get more comfortable with showing her feelings, or undermine her own success.

Common push-pull pairings to look for are:

(PULL) Direct revelation of new information results in...
(PUSH) A change in strategy.

(PULL) A physical action changes the situation, resulting in...(PUSH) A shift in power.

(PULL) An outside interruption or force of nature results in...(PUSH) An addition or subtraction.

Dwight Swain in *Techniques of the Selling Writer* explains that every scene containing a goal, motivation, and conflict ends in one of four ways: "Yes," "No," "Yes, but...it comes at a price the character isn't prepared to pay," or "No, and furthermore...the character is worse off than before."

The same is true of sequences. While all four possible resolutions have their place, only two are capable of driving the story and increasing the stakes. They are "Yes, but..." and "No, and furthermore..." A simple "Yes" or "No" resolves the tension and stops the story, which is why they are reserved to answer the major story goal at the end.

For the first half of the story, events are the big "Yes, but..." or "No, and furthermore..." scene ending each sequence and swinging the whole story in a new direction. The character scrambles to respond to the "Yes, but..." or "No, and furthermore..." event with a new goal and purpose, thus launching upon a new sequence. Which culminates in a new "Yes, but..." or "No, and furthermore..." event, which launches a new sequence, etc. And so on, until the middle of the story. Then the order of things switches around. Events come first, challenging the protagonist with questions. Sequences chart the fallout and consequences of each event, answering "Yes, but..." or "No, and furthermore...," until the end of the story, where the final sequence depicts either a "Yes," or "No."

In the previous example of the bank robbery thriller, a "Yes, but..." event resolving the "whittling down opponents" sequence might be that the protagonist succeeds at taking out some of the bank robbers, but as a result of the mayhem that ensues is himself mistaken by the authorities as one of the bad guys. Which creates a new sequence goal of proving his identity and loyalty to the cops on the case so he won't become the target of friendly fire.

The "Yes, but…" and "No, and furthermore…" events are also great ways to weave together throughlines. The "Yes" part can apply to one throughline, while the consequences of the "but…" part fall out in another throughline. Or the "No" part answers one throughline, while the "and furthermore…" part plays out in another throughline. For example, in the thriller story referenced earlier, the "Yes" part of the event applies to the External Throughline, where the protagonist is trying to stop the bank robbers. The "but it comes at a price …" part crosses over into the Relationship Throughline where the protagonist's developing friendship with one of the cops is jeopardized. In the above example from *The Hunger Games*, the sequence sets up the External Throughline question, "Can Katniss and Peeta leverage their training to win public support?" The event of Peeta's public declaration braids Relationship and Internal Throughlines into the answer. "Yes, but it turns an unwelcome spotlight on Katniss's emotions and personal relationships."

This utilization of events to cross throughlines is a key part of "teaching" the protagonist via demonstration ("show, don't tell") the consequences of both his fatal flaw and changed behavior as the story progresses. He may take one step forward in one throughline, only to discover his behavior has taken him two steps backwards in another throughline.

The Story Skeleton

Just as the human skeleton enables a person to stand upright, so structure empowers a story to stand on its own two feet. Sequences are the bones, events the joints, that give a story shape in readers' imaginations. Visualizing story structure as a skeleton, it's easy to comprehend the organic connection and natural progression of its various parts.

One leg is the first Act, joined to the torso of Act Two at the hip. The other leg is Act Three. Now imagine a center dividing line from head to toe, distinguishing the first and second halves of Act Two. Presiding over the apex of Act Two's parts is the head, the midpoint reversal.

The story begins when the foot of Act One touches down on the first page, and concludes when the foot of Act Three rests solidly on the last page. Straddling the pages in-between are the joints and bones of the intervening events and sequences.

Starting at Act One and progressing up one side of the body to the head, and then down the other side to the final leg of Act Three reveals an organic flow of connectivity. Just as specific bones and joints are designed to fit together, so specific sequences fit together, creating form and context. The setup sequence is connected to the stakes sequence, and the stakes sequence is connected to the...etc. One leads naturally into the next. Skip one or try to connect a shin bone to a shoulder blade, and the entire skeleton collapses.

In the following section are brief descriptions of the sequences and events to look for when X-raying any novel for plot, conflict, and character. Examples include some spoilers. If you are unfamiliar with any of the following novels, you may desire to temporarily skip over their examples until such time as you've had opportunity to read the novels in full. They are highly recommended, both for education and pleasure.

The Alaskan, by James Oliver Curwood. An example of a romance where the love interest serves the dual function of primary antagonist, and there's also a villain. This prolific historical romance writer was the bestselling and highest paid author of his time. Amazon offers the free ebook, and sells paperback and hardcover editions. Also, Project Gutenberg has the free ebook in various formats.

Jessica's First Prayer, by Hesba Stretton. An example of a drama where the non-romantic love interest also functions as primary antagonist, and there is no villain. Stretton's first novel (out of more than 40) sold over 1.5 million copies during her lifetime. Amazon offers the ebook for $0.99, and sells paperback and hardcover editions. Also, archive.org has the free ebook in various formats.

Tarzan of the Apes, by Edgar Rice Burroughs. An example of an adventure story heavily laced with coming-of-age elements and a strong romantic subplot. Superlative to any Tarzan movie adaptation ever filmed. Amazon offers the free ebook, and sells paperback and hardcover editions. Also, Project Gutenberg has the free ebook in various formats.

The Leg Bone Connected To The...

Here is a map of the eight sequences and their correlating events that make up every successful story. They are numbered according to their order of occurrence. In the first half of the story, each sequence builds toward a punctuating event. In the last half of the story, a catalyzing event initiates each sequence. There are two sequences in Act One, four sequences in Act Two, and two sequences in Act Three.

STORY SKELETON

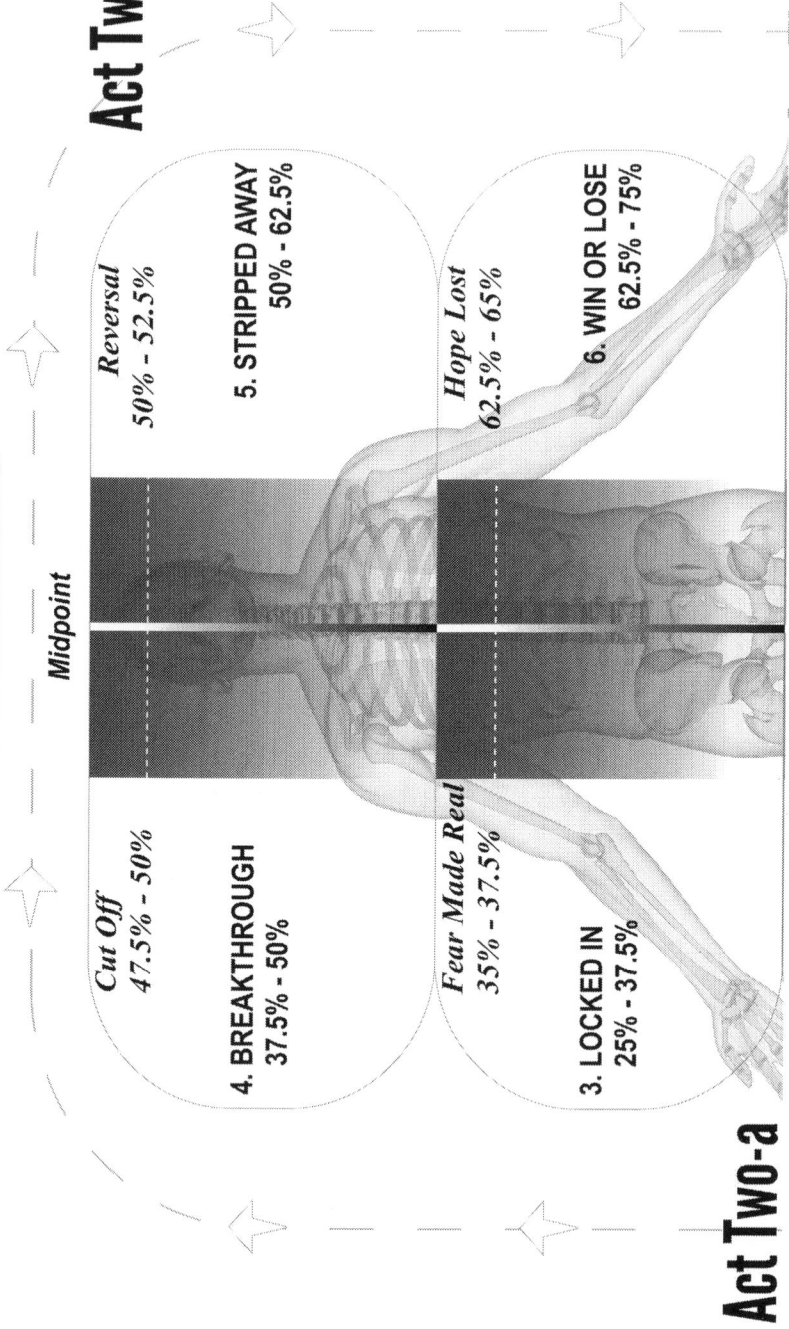

Act Two-b

Reversal
50% - 52.5%

5. STRIPPED AWAY
50% - 62.5%

Hope Lost
62.5% - 65%

6. WIN OR LOSE
62.5% - 75%

Midpoint

Cut Off
47.5% - 50%

4. BREAKTHROUGH
37.5% - 50%

Fear Made Real
35% - 37.5%

3. LOCKED IN
25% - 37.5%

Act Two-a

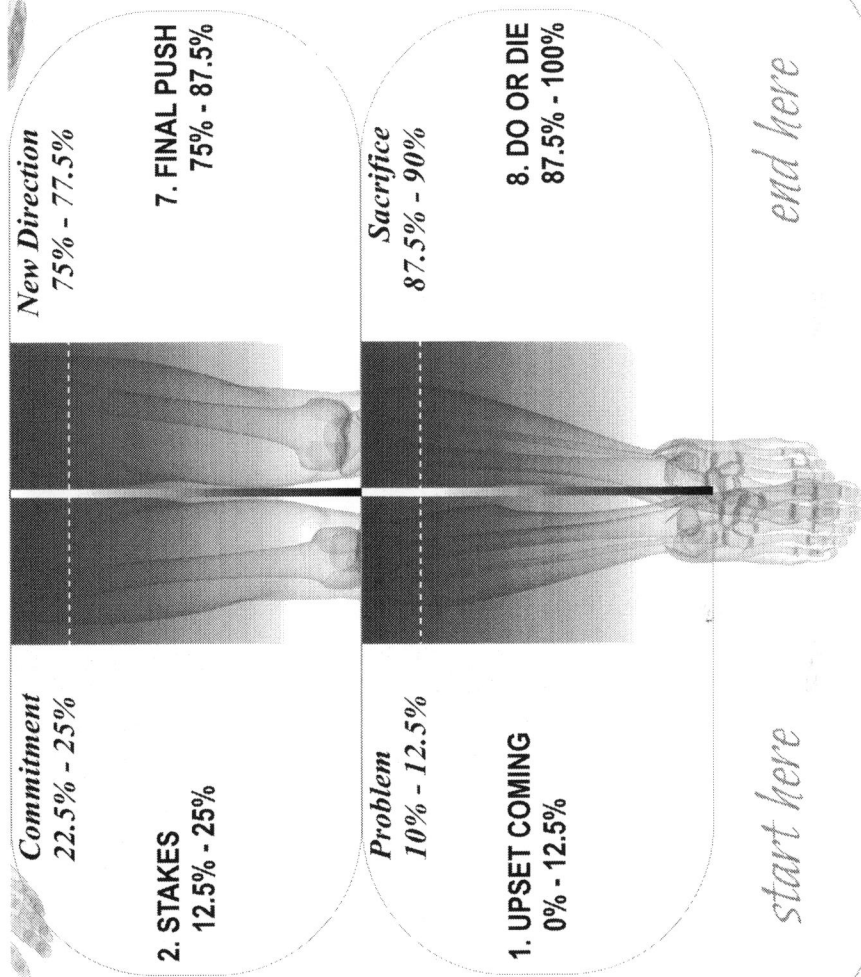

Sequences

1. Upset Coming (0% - 12.5%) / *Culminating Event: Problem (10% - 12.5%)*
2. Stakes (12.5% - 25%) / *Culminating Event: Commitment (22.5% - 25%)*
3. Locked in (25% - 37.5%) / *Culminating Event: Fear Made Real (35% - 37.5%)*
4. Breakthrough (37.5% - 50%) / *Culminating Event: Cut Off (47.5% - 50%)*
5. *Initiating Event: Reversal (50% - 52.5%)* / Stripped Away (50% - 62.5%)
6. *Initiating Event: Hope Lost (62.5% - 65%)* / Win or Lose (62.5% - 75%)
7. *Initiating Event: New Direction (75% - 77.5%)* / Final Push (75% - 87.5%)
8. *Initiating Event: Sacrifice (87.5% - 90%)* / Do or Die (87.5% - 100%)

A printable version of the above Story Skeleton is available as a FREE download for anyone who has purchased this book. Please visit the following website for more information and other *free* bonus material: marymercer.weebly.com.

Act One

First Sequence — Upset Coming (0% - 12.5%) — This opening sequence starts with the moment the protagonist's life changes, except he doesn't understand why he's feeling uneasy. Even in stories that open with a "bang!", the jolt to the main character's life remains deliberately unacknowledged on a core psychological level. "I'm jilted at the altar, kidnapped by aliens, and buried alive in the Arctic, but I don't have to change how I respond to life!" He's still trying to juggle his life the same way he always has, but he's already losing his grip on his comfort zone. The equilibrium of his life is slipping rapidly through his fingers, and he can feel it. Restrictions are beginning to chafe and his sense of security fray. Still he's in denial that things are changing, or that he can't get them back to the way they were before.

Scenes in this sequence often touch on the three primary areas of the protagonist's life: his private life at home, his personal life with friends, and his professional life at work. Something is lacking in these areas, and though he's not ready to admit it, his flaw is what's causing him problems.

To invest the reader in the drama surrounding the protagonist's choices, the motivation is best established in the context of powerful emotions, such as faith, hope, love, envy, jealousy, or greed. Likewise, the moral dilemma is most powerful when opposing options exert an equally strong push-pull on the protagonist. He wants something dearly (pulling him toward a certain anticipated outcome), but he's equally afraid of something else (pushing him away from the same outcome).

This sequence is Point A in the protagonist's character arc to Point B at the end. It's significant because it provides contrast and thus a way to measure the character's growth, which means change, which means satisfying a reader's reason for reading the story.

Identifying Characteristics—

- ▸ Establishes the protagonist's Internal Throughline, the driving need that will propel him through the rest of the story.
- ▸ Introduces the protagonist in a manner that invites reader identification and empathy.
- ▸ Establishes the protagonist's strengths that will pay off later in the story. (Ex: in a thriller, the FBI agent hero may be shown here practicing expert marksmanship at the firing range.)
- ▸ Introduces the antagonist/villain, or at least his representative, in a way that demonstrates the threat of his strength or cunning.

▸ Shows the protagonist's fear, wound, or flawed belief as it relates to the Relationship Throughline.

▸ Introduces, either directly or indirectly, all of the main characters in accordance with their primary thematic roles in the story.

▸ A line of dialogue addresses the theme, often by a character other than the protagonist and directed to the protagonist. "You know what your problem is? You're too..."

▸ Sometimes begins with a "hook"—a tense scene that grabs the reader's interest, cleverly characterizing the protagonist, but doesn't feed directly into the dominant throughline of the story.

Other names for this sequence: Status Quo; the Setup (Snyder) (Hauge); The Ordinary World (Vogler); the Chemical Equation: Setup (Mernit); Dependent World/Price of Conformity (Hudson); "I Don't Get No Respect" (Schechter).

EXAMPLES

The Alaskan, by James Oliver Curwood – When Mary Standish elects coldly cynical pioneer Alan Holt as her escort aboard the *Nome*, her nearness jolts his stoicism. She's looking for a man to trust and believe in, but his love for Alaska and hatred of financial giant John Graham are his only passions.

Jessica's First Prayer, by Hesba Stretton – An elderly, secretive operator of a coffee-stall near the railway bridge has compassion on a starving and threadbare little girl, giving her food and a seat by the fire.

Tarzan of the Apes, by Edgar Rice Burroughs – Newlyweds Lord Greystoke and Lady Alice, en route to a British diplomatic posting, are stranded by mutineers on the untamed coast of darkest Africa. Their struggle for survival against jungle and beasts is punctuated by the birth of their son and the death of Lady Alice.

First Sequence's Culminating Event — Problem (10% - 12.5%) —

This is the event that directly challenges the protagonist's fatal flaw. A fatal flaw is a lie, a fear, or a weakness that the character clings to because he erroneously believes it's protecting him or making life, if not better, at least manageable. It's really ruining his life, but he doesn't see it that way. It's the *real* reason he was jilted at the altar, kidnapped by aliens, and buried alive in the Arctic.

This event isn't always bad news. Sometimes the "problem" arrives cloaked as a golden opportunity. It can sound like good news, but whether it's a promotion or a pink slip, the protagonist can't properly respond to it without changing. And therein beats the heart of the Problem event.

The key to this event is that it forces the protagonist to make an immediate decision. Usually that decision is an attempt to save or preserve his fatal flaw. Though he doesn't know it yet, it's his first small step toward change, because his fatal flaw is no longer sufficient to maintain the status quo. He has to reach beyond that flaw for the answer, even though at this point he has no intention of permanently changing.

In romance novels, it's encouraged to have the hero and heroine physically meet as close to the first page, or even first sentence, as possible. But this event is where the relationship gets down to business. This is where the romantic hero and heroine first cross swords over the central conflict of the story. They may have sparred in the earlier scenes of the sequence, but this is the event that hits closer to home, that promises to define the nature of their relationship conflict for the rest of the book. (For example, a secret baby story, or a marriage of convenience tale, or a runaway bride book, etc.)

Identifying Characteristics—

- Catapults the protagonist out of his dysfunctional comfort zone.
- Something external that happens *to* the protagonist. Often initiated or driven by the antagonist.
- Often takes the form of the arrival of bad news, or even seemingly good news. Sometimes an arrival or departure of another character. Either way, it *always* heralds significant change.
- If the previous sequence focused on a problem in a subplot, the protagonist may initially welcome this Problem event as the seeming solution.
- Not an internal realization. Naval gazing doesn't count here. The protagonist is too stuck in his old ways to listen to a still, small voice.
- The protagonist makes a decision.

Other names for this event: Catalyst (Snyder); Call to Adventure (Vogler); Turning Point #1: The Opportunity (Hauge); Cute Meet: Catalyst (Mernit); Inciting Incident (Field); Opportunity to Shine (Hudson); "Do You Know What Your Trouble Is?" (Schechter).

EXAMPLES

The Alaskan, by James Oliver Curwood – Alan becomes "involved in spite of himself" when he catches Mary in an apparent midnight tryst with Rossland, one of John Graham's agents.

Jessica's First Prayer, by Hesba Stretton – Little Jessica wishes she could stay at the coffee-stall, where it's warm and pleasant. The cautious coffee-stall operator relents to allow her return the following week for a single meal, under strict conditions.

Tarzan of the Apes, by Edgar Rice Burroughs – The great apes attack and kill Lord Greystoke, but his infant son is rescued and adopted by a female ape recently bereft of her own baby.

Second Sequence — Stakes (12.5% - 25%) — The final sequence of Act One establishes the physical and emotional stakes in the story. Two sides of the theme are argued here, for and against, that set the stage for everything that follows. Two opposing beliefs in a tug of war, with the protagonist caught in the middle. Often the protagonist initially refuses whatever the Problem event challenged him to do. However, just as often he doesn't refuse at all. He's eager to meet the challenge head on, believing his decision from the Problem event will easily solve his problem. But this sequence proves he's up against more than he bargained for.

An important component of this sequence often takes the shape of a Mentor archetype. A Mentor can be good and kind, guiding the protagonist with pure intentions. Or the Mentor can be shifty, selfish, tricking the protagonist into a decision merely to set him up for defeat later on. In any case, it's a role imbued with trust, either earned or misplaced.

In a romance, this is the sequence where the hero or heroine rebuffs the love interest. The doubts and fears focus on how incompatible they are. The Mentor might take the form of good friends encouraging them to give the relationship a shot, or well-intentioned but misguided friends warning them against getting involved.

Identifying Characteristics—

- Doubts and fears expressed about the cost of continuing. Either the protagonist's doubts and fears, or someone else's who is trying to make him come to his senses before it's too late. What does the protagonist hope to gain? What is he terrified of losing?
- The protagonist's relationship with the love interest or else the love interest herself is put at risk or in jeopardy, often due to the antagonist/villain.
- The protagonist's options are debated until they are crystal clear.
- The first superficial layer of the protagonist's motivations are explored. He remains largely unaware of his own deeper, subtler reasons to resist change.
- Early taste of the bigger obstacles ahead.
- A Mentor character, embodying one side of the theme, prepares the protagonist in some way to make the decisive leap into Act Two.
- The last opportunity to introduce major characters.

Other names for this sequence: Debate (Snyder); Refusal of the Call/Meeting with the Mentor (Vogler); the New Situation (Hauge); Dresses the Part (Hudson); Calls and Busy Signals (Schechter).

EXAMPLES

The Alaskan, by James Oliver Curwood – Alan's cynical preconceptions about women are shattered as Mary gets under his skin, despite contradictory evidence she may be holding secret assignations with Rossland aboard ship.

Jessica's First Prayer, by Hesba Stretton – Jessica's contrite confession to stealing a penny smites Daniel's conscience, for he knows he is not a "very good man" as she insists and would have kept it himself. Wednesday breakfasts together become their routine.

Tarzan of the Apes, by Edgar Rice Burroughs – Tarzan grows up a hated misfit among his ape tribe, though loved by his ape mother. Discovering an abandoned cabin stocked with English-language books, he begins a journey of knowledge, and grows into a mighty killer.

Second Sequence's Culminating Event — **Commitment (22.5% - 25%)** — The antagonist raises the stakes, compelling the protagonist to decide on a plan of action or put the plan hashed out in the sequence into action. The dramatic power of this moment is found in the certainty of the protagonist's purpose. He *intentionally* commits to carry out his plan. No one deceives or pushes him into it or makes the decision for him. He owns it, clearly asserting what he wants to win, gain, or achieve.

This decision applies increased pressure on the protagonist's flaw, because even while it seems to reaffirm that his flaw works to his benefit, this event simultaneously forces him to compromise in a key area. The protagonist is like a little kid who, while deciding to obey in body, remains stubbornly rebellious in spirit. "I may be sitting down on the outside, but I'm still standing up on the inside." For example, if he's a lone wolf, he still erroneously believes at this point he's better off alone, but this event forces him to take on a partner and do things differently to make any progress toward his goal.

Because this is one of the points in the story where the protagonist's external and internal worlds powerfully collide, this event plays out in one of two different ways in a romance. If there's nothing internal really in the way of the hero and heroine's happily ever after, then their external goals generate the conflict. But if no huge external conflicts exist, then either the hero or heroine (or both!) wrestle with internal conflicts keeping them apart. Either way, this is the event where the protagonist is forced to acknowledge to herself the attraction between them is real, it's serious. It's also the event that forces them to spend time together for the rest of the book. For example, if the heroine has been pestering the hero to be her guide on a wilderness adventure, this is the event where he finally agrees, but it's also where she realizes the attraction between them is a direct threat to her inner fear, flaw, wound, or belief.

Identifying Characteristics—

- The protagonist is locked into the central conflict of the story heralded by the Problem event.
- The protagonist intentionally decides to join the central conflict for his own sake. No one else makes this decision for him.
- Creates a "new world" of circumstances he's never dealt with before.
- Often depicted metaphorically as a significant change in location, seasons, or weather. Can be as simple as the protagonist crossing through a doorway.
- In a mystery, the detective commences actively investigating the crime.

▸ In a romance, the hero and heroine are bound together from this point forward in a significant, inescapable way that lays bare simmering attractions.

Other names for this event: Break Into Two (Snyder); Crossing the First Threshold (Vogler); Turning Point #2: the Change of Plans (Hauge); A Sexy Complication: Turning Point (Mernit); Plot Point #1 (Field); the Secret World (Hudson); Through the Looking Glass (Schechter).

EXAMPLES

The Alaskan, by James Oliver Curwood – Mary secretly appeals to Alan to help her stage her own death... Or else she must really die. She cannot reach their destination alive. Deciding she's a liar or a fool, he refuses.

Jessica's First Prayer, by Hesba Stretton – Jessica spots Daniel on the street, and surreptitiously follows him inside a church, which is like a fairyland to her. Much to his anxiety and dismay, someone now knows his secret double-life as a respected church-keeper.

Tarzan of the Apes, by Edgar Rice Burroughs – Tarzan kills his lifelong ape enemy in hand-to-hand combat, and desires to set himself apart as a man clothed.

Act Two — first half

Third Sequence — Locked In (25% - 37.5%) — The protagonist's old ways of doing things and old beliefs don't work anymore. Old allies might turn into enemies, or supposed enemies prove to be good friends. This could be as simple as well-intentioned friends giving bad advice, or as complex as Machiavellian political intrigues. This sequence is actually where the creative concept of the whole story is often played out. Blake Snyder refers to the "Promise of the Premise." For example, if it's a romance novel about a minimum-wage waitress who falls in love with a tenured literature professor, then this is where she tries to fit into his stuffy intellectual world and he meets her rowdy football-loving family. It's where what sold the reader on the story comes true. It's the meat of the backcover blurb.

Readers expect the protagonist to take the most logical course of action in pursuit of his goal, the most logical also promising to be the easiest, simplest, or quickest solution. It's human nature. This obvious choice will hang suspended like a guillotine blade over the credibility of the story until it is addressed. Protagonists defend themselves against possible charges of being "too stupid to live" by trying and discarding those options here.

In a thriller, amateur sleuth mystery, or any story where the protagonist's first natural recourse would be to appeal to the lawful authorities for aid or protection, this sequence is where that happens. He seeks out the cops, expecting to find allies, only to discover that for their own reasons they are not. If they were, the story would end prematurely.

Sometimes, the protagonist's backstory rears its ugly head here, blocking him from accepting the help readily available to him or from taking the road most travelled. The backstory needn't be explained in detail at this point, so long as its power as an obstacle (an "internal enemy" of sorts) is apparent.

Identifying Characteristics—

- New minor or supporting characters may be introduced.
- The protagonist implements the first and easiest plan to solve the story problem.

- The protagonist solicits the assistance of new allies and wrestles against new enemies. ("New" refers to their position as helper or opponent to his plan, not the length of their acquaintance.)
- The protagonist's appeals for help from the most likely sources are blocked or turned down.
- The protagonist rejects the most obvious solution or source of help because of his internal flaw, fear, or wrong belief.
- Sometimes the protagonist undertakes training in preparation to implementing his plan.
- A subplot kicks into high gear.
- In a romance, this is often the "getting to know you" stage where the hero and heroine become acquainted with each others's flaws and strengths.
- A deadline or "ticking clock" may appear, exerting increasing pressure on the protagonist to take urgent action.

Other names for this sequence: Fun and Games (Snyder); Tests, Allies, and Enemies (Vogler); Progress (Hauge); No Longer Fits Her World (Hudson); Kick the Dog (Schechter).

EXAMPLES

The Alaskan, by James Oliver Curwood – The next morning, Mary is reported gone overboard and presumed dead. Driven by responsibility for her death, Alan commences a desperate search and recovery mission.

Jessica's First Prayer, by Hesba Stretton – Daniel drives Jessica out of the church before anyone sees, but her curiosity about prayer and God inspire her to shrewdly find ways to sneak back inside every Sunday.

Tarzan of the Apes, by Edgar Rice Burroughs – Cannibals slay Tarzan's ape mother, and his vengeance leads him back to their camp. He discovers much practical knowledge from his first encounter with mankind, enabling him to become King of the Apes.

Third Sequence's Culminating Event — Fear Made Real (35% - 37.5%) — Just when the protagonist may be flagging in his new purpose or plan, this external event comes along to kick him in the rear, get him going again, and keep him on track. Often, although not always, it's the antagonist doing the kicking. At a minimum, it's an antagonist force. This event often ties a major throughline back into the first sequence's Problem event. The protagonist had a plan, but now it's abruptly changed, and his motivation is tested. Because he realizes he no longer fits into the old world of Act One, he is forced to react in a new way.

By providing a quick look at the protagonist's greatest fear or weakness, this event raises the stakes and sets up the danger of the climactic confrontation later in Act Three. It could be as simple as defining the principals and/or the principles who will face off later, or as complex as a detailed preview of the showdown ahead. In Suzanne Collins' *The Hunger Games*, the Locked In sequence showed Katniss' and Peeta's training and preparation in the Capitol for the Games. At the conclusion of their training, they are given interviews. Public support, a vital component of survival in the Games, hinges on giving a good performance. Katniss barely squeaks by. Then comes the culminating event, and it's Peeta's turn. He reveals he's in love, but it probably won't work out since the girl is Katniss! This is her Fear Made Real, because Katniss' focus on strength makes her really awkward with gentler emotions. It's already been established her mother suffered an emotional breakdown because of a relationship that ended badly, becoming too weak to provide for her kids who depended on her. Yet Peeta's revelation forces Katniss to make a decision. In order to succeed in the Games, she must play along with the idea of a hopeless love affair whose very nature terrifies her (internal principles in conflict), and which will probably end in her or Peeta killing each other in the arena (external principals in conflict).

While a mystery may use this event to imprint on the reader the physical danger involved, other stories may use it to setup emotional jeopardy. In a romance, this may be where the couple experiences their first quarrel, thus realizing a level of emotional danger to their hearts. In a thriller, it might be when a lesser supporting character stumbles into the villain's clutches and dies.

Identifying Characteristics—

- The emotional or physical danger of pursuing his goal is experienced by the protagonist in a way that makes it close and personal as never before.
- The protagonist comes face-to-face with his greatest fear or weakness.
- The love interest in the Relationship Throughline is emotionally or physically threatened, thus raising the stakes.
- The protagonist is forced to renew his commitment to his goal.
- Establishes the antagonist's commitment to his goal, and the strength of his motivation.

▸ Sometimes the arrival or departure of an important or unexpected ally makes the protagonist newly aware of his own vulnerability and slim chance of success alone.

Other names for this event: Pinch Point #1 (Fields).

EXAMPLES

The Alaskan, by James Oliver Curwood – Alan is forced to abandon the search for Mary's body, admitting at last that something stronger than guilt drove him. Despite the brevity of their acquaintance, he loved her.

Jessica's First Prayer, by Hesba Stretton – The minister's children discover Jessica hiding in the church.

Tarzan of the Apes, by Edgar Rice Burroughs – Tarzan defeats a challenger to his throne, Terkoz, but in the way of rational man lets him live. Renouncing the ways of the apes, he takes "his first step toward the goal which he had set," and leaves to find civilized men.

Fourth Sequence — Breakthrough (37.5% - 50%) — The alliances formed in the previous Locked In sequence are tested again by setbacks in this sequence. Bonds are formed and strengthened, or strained and crack apart. There is a sense of forward momentum, as the protagonist has the antagonist in his sights and is closing in for a major confrontation.

The previous sequence saw the protagonist trying the easiest and simplest approach to solve his problem. The Fear Made Real event saw that effort fail in a way that cost him something precious, or he got an up-close look at his greatest fear. Either way, the stakes have been raised. Now he comes up with a new plan and tries even harder to reach his goal. Or, if the previous sequence showed the protagonist training and preparing to put his original plan into action, this is where he actually attempts to carry it out.

Identifying Characteristics—

- The protagonist designs and carries out a new plan to achieve his goal.
- The protagonist tries to "get inside the skin" of his opponent by seeking to understand the antagonist's plan (yes, he has one, too!). Usually this plan is explained in dialogue delivered by or to the protagonist.
- The protagonist believes he has all the pieces of the puzzle, or thinks he knows everything he needs to know in order to win, obtain, or achieve what he wants.
- The protagonist finds out who his true allies are when the going gets tough, as power struggles erupt and fairweather friends scramble for the exits.
- The bond between the protagonist and love interest in the Relationship Throughline deepens and strengthens.

Other names for this sequence: Fun and Games - continued (Snyder); Approach to the Inmost Cave (Vogler); Which Way is Up? (Schechter).

EXAMPLES

The Alaskan, by James Oliver Curwood – Alan travels alone across the vast Alaskan tundra, and in a fever-haze of grief hallucinates Mary is beside him and returns his love. Arriving home at his reindeer range, he finds her alive and awaiting him.

Jessica's First Prayer, by Hesba Stretton – Scared Daniel will find out and she'll lose his friendship, but also driven to find out about God, Jessica allows the minister and his children to take her under their wing.

Tarzan of the Apes, by Edgar Rice Burroughs – A ship arrives on the coast of Africa, marooning a group of hapless adventurers on the beach. Tarzan watches from a distance and wonders at the strange newcomers, among whom is the beautiful American, Jane Porter.

Fourth Sequence's Culminating Event — Cut Off (47.5% - 50%) — This event and the next immediately following binds the protagonist and antagonist together in a way that neither can ever turn back from again. Thus, the stakes are raised to incredible new heights. This one-two punch spins the protagonist and the story in a new direction, often reversing roles.

During the Breakthrough sequence, the protagonist put his plan into action. Now when he believes he's got victory in his sights, he finds himself unexpectedly cut off at the pass. Sometimes this is literal, as in Daniel Dafoe's *Robinson Crusoe* when the title character's attempt to sail around the island is literally cut off by a wall of rock jutting into the sea. Other times a character's best laid plans are cut off by unexpected emotional currents. In the movie *People Will Talk*, the protagonist physician (Cary Grant) is cut off by complicated family dynamics from revealing an unwed pregnancy to the girl's doting father. In stories where the main character's arc is less about change and more about clinging to defined values, it may be the protagonist who cuts off the antagonist. As in David Thompson's *Comanche Moon*, when the honorable hero of the long-running *Wilderness* series, Nate King, cuts off a married woman's advances.

Sometimes the protagonist is not only cut off but trapped, as in Suzanne Collins' *The Hunger Games* when the Careers trap Katniss up in the tree. Or a trap may be revealed to be a cleverly disguised rescue. The protagonist himself may attempt to set a trap for the antagonist/villain, as in Vera Caspary's *Laura*.

In thrillers or mysteries, this is often where the villain attacks and bodies drop. A classic example is when the detective's prime suspect becomes the real murderer's latest victim. In well-crafted stories, this isn't for shock effect. The attack makes a difference by reversing roles and forcing characters to adapt to ever increasing stakes. For example, in C.S. Lewis's *The Lion, the Witch, and the Wardrobe*, Edmund "attacks" his siblings by deliberately betraying their location to the White Witch.

Almost always the fourth sequence's culminating event provides the protagonist and the reader with a glimpse of how the story might resolve. It may be true or false. It may be what they hope will happen or what they fear will happen. But it is not the real resolution because not all the pieces of the dramatic puzzle are in place. In romances, this is often where a stolen kiss or magical date gives the protagonist an important peek at not only true love's wonders but also his or her own internal growth destination. It's "stolen" because the character has yet to complete the inner growth required to earn and sustain a happy ending. Sometimes what the protagonist sees isn't pretty. Perhaps the protagonist gets an unhappy glimpse of his own flaws and inadequacies, and ends the romance out of despair love can ever work out. In Robert Heinlein's science fiction classic *The Puppet Masters*, the protagonist gets an up-close-and-personal look at a city saturated with alien invaders. Whether it's full of hope or rife with fear, the protagonist tastes and sees what change can feel like, thus strengthening his or her motivation for the hard work ahead.

Glimpses can take the shape of experiences in the present or dialogue about the past or future. Experiences are always more profound than dialogue, because the former is "showing" while the latter is "telling." For this reason "telling" glimpses are often doubled up with "showing" glimpses for maximum impact. In James Oliver Curwood's *The Flaming Forest*, the hero describes a fugitive's horrific crime to the heroine (false glimpse, since it turns out he didn't possess all the facts). Later, he and the heroine embrace in an experiential taste of love (true glimpse, since it's a romance with a happy ending). If a glimpse is told *by* the protagonist *to* another character, it's often unwittingly false, because the protagonist's arc at this point in incomplete. But if another character is doing the telling, it's often true and challenges the protagonist's belief system, as in Lisa Kleypas's *Smooth-Talking Stranger*, when Jack describes the perfect date to Ella, giving her a glimpse of what a relationship with him would be like.

Identifying Characteristics—

- The protagonist's plan fails horribly, often because he lacked essential information. Instead, a world-changing revelation cuts him off from reaching his goal.
- The protagonist comes face-to-face with the antagonist, and is forced to re-examine his view of the world and everything that's happened.
- The protagonist may be trapped by or sets a trap for the antagonist/villain.
- The protagonist either appears to die, witnesses death, or causes death. The "death" here can be physical or emotional (example: the death of a goal, an illusion, a defense mechanism, a relationship, etc.)

- The protagonist glimpses a possible outcome to the story, and is forced to face either his highest hopes (by experimenting with internal growth) or worst fears (by surrendering to despair at his own flaws).
- A deadline or "ticking clock" is about to go off.
- The antagonist or villain attacks.
- A trap is set, either by the protagonist for the antagonist/villain, or by the antagonist/villain for the protagonist.
- Often in mysteries, either the prime suspect is exonerated by an ironclad alibi or is found dead, shattering the detective's carefully constructed theories and flawed assumptions. He is forced to push past his own flaws and turn in a new direction to solve the crime.
- In a romance, this is often (okay, almost always) the Big Love Scene, where the protagonist's defenses against love die and his heart is exposed.
- Or, in a romance, if the protagonist comes face-to-face with his worst fear (such as betrayal, abandonment, or disappointment) and freaks out, it's the Big Breakup.

Other names for this event: Midpoint (Snyder) (Field); The Supreme Ordeal (Vogler); Turning Point #3: the Point of No Return (Hauge); The Hook: Midpoint (Mernit); Gives Up What Kept Her Stuck (Hudson); When Life Gives You Lemons... (Schechter).

EXAMPLES
The Alaskan, by James Oliver Curwood – With an honorable expression of sincere friendship and trust in him, Mary cuts off Alan's foolish dreams of love.

Jessica's First Prayer, by Hesba Stretton – To Daniel's intense anxiety and displeasure, the minister seats Jessica in front of the pulpit for Sunday service.

Tarzan of the Apes, by Edgar Rice Burroughs – A lioness attacks Jane in Lord and Lady Greystoke's abandoned cabin. Tarzan attacks and kills the lioness with his bare hands, saving Jane's life, though she only catches a glimpse of him.

Midpoint

The Midpoint marks a perceptible change in energy and direction in the story. It is a dramatic dividing line right down the middle. Everything that comes after it mirrors what came before, revealing new depths of character as roles are reversed. The hunter becomes the hunted. The suspect becomes the victim. The love interest becomes the romantic pursuer. For example, in the first half of *North and South* by Elizabeth Gaskell, the heroine surprises the hero over and over again in circumstances reflecting badly on him and which he's helpless to explain. He suffers her rejection for it. After the Midpoint, their roles reverse as he catches her over and over again in compromising circumstances she can't explain. It's her turn to experience the same suffering he endured earlier, and her admiration for him grows after "walking in his shoes."

An important element of this role reversal involves the protagonist's flawed goal. Up until the Midpoint, he believed his goal represented the solution to his problem. At the Midpoint, he acknowledges a new and worthy goal (often involving the Relationship Throughline), and suddenly the flawed goal *becomes* the problem to ever attaining the new goal. As in the movie *While You Were Sleeping*. Lucy's loneliness and longing for family motivated her to develop the flawed goal of marrying her Dream Prince, Peter. It seems to solve all her problems... for awhile, so long as she can maintain the lie that they're engaged. At the Midpoint, she realizes she's falling in love with her Real Prince, Jack. Suddenly her flawed goal *becomes* the problem to ever attaining her new and worthy goal of real love with Jack. As long as he believes she's engaged to his brother, he'll never betray his family's happiness.

Up to this point in the story's structure, sequences developed from scenes building toward a defined climactic event, which triggered another sequence that built toward its own climactic event, and so on. Beginning with the fifth sequence, that pattern changes and turns on its head. From now on, each sequence's key event occurs at the beginning, with subsequent scenes dealing with the aftermath of that event.

This transition in pattern from sequence-event to event-sequence creates a rare collision in the middle of the story. For the first and only time two events butt up against one another. The fourth sequence's culminating event and the fifth sequence's initiating event together create the major turning point reversal known as the Midpoint. These back-to-back events create a dynamic twist in the story, powered by the driving force of rapid chain-reaction decisions braiding together different throughlines. Because of a decision at the fourth sequence's culminating event, another decision must be made immediately in another throughline at the beginning of the fifth sequence. It's a simple matter of cause and effect. A character decided *this*, as a consequence of which another character decides *that*. For example, in C.S. Lewis's *The Lion, the Witch and the Wardrobe*, the fourth sequence's culminating event is Edmund's betrayal of his siblings and Aslan to the White Witch. The fifth sequence's initiating event is the siblings' resulting decision to flee to Aslan at the Stone Table.

Decisions only impact story structure when they are transformed into action. A character may think of doing something, anticipate doing it, even prepare to do it, but it's not until he actually does it that it counts. After all, he might change his mind or something unforeseen interfere. That's why the decisions that mark events are almost always immediately expressed as tangible actions. It's an important component of the old adage, "Show, don't tell." A decision isn't really truly made until it's carried out and can't be rescinded. In that sense, readers register decisions the moment a character acts. Everything that may have gone before, dithering, speculation, determination, etc., primes the reader's anticipation but cannot convince where action is not present. However, sometimes lengthening the time between decision and action can elevate tension. For example, in *The Lion, the Witch, and the Wardrobe* the possibility of Edmund's betrayal and the siblings' need to flee arises in the middle of the fourth sequence. (Will he go through with it? Will his brother and sisters escape in time? Tension develops as the pages turn to find out.) But the actual *act* of betrayal occurs at the culminating event. And the siblings' actual rush out the door ahead of the White Witch happens immediately afterwards at the initiating event of the fifth sequence.

Act Two — second half

Fifth Sequence's Initiating Event — Reversal (50% - 52.5%) — After being cut off in the previous event, the protagonist has questions about what went wrong and often takes action here in pursuit of answers. If the heroine caught a glimpse of happiness with her prince, the answers she seeks may be from a friend or mentor on how to catch a man. The hero may want answers about a possible rival for his lady's affections. Or if the hero dumped her, the heroine may track him down to demand an explanation. In mysteries, this is often where the detectives gather the witnesses for questioning and a significant clue arises but is initially shelved or overlooked.

Earlier in the third sequence, the protagonist's backstory may have blocked him from reaching out for help, but it wasn't explained. This event is one of two possible places in the story where it can work to have detailed or emotionally complex backstory revealed. Any sooner, and it would bore a reader to sleep. The key to backstory is that the reveal is not about the information from the *past*. It's about internal conflict and character growth in the *present*. This information is something the character kept close to the vest for a reason. Sharing it at this point, probably with the love interest character in the Relationship Throughline, is a choice to make himself vulnerable. He wants the other character to understand him better so the relationship can grow closer. It's a step of faith. So while the backstory here answers urgent questions that surfaced in the last event, the act of trust involved in revealing it to the other character kicks off a whole new sequence. In James Oliver Curwood's *The Hunted Woman*, the heroine reveals to the hero horrific details of her marriage. Realizing she's not grieving her late husband but rather is relieved at being free, he sets out to win her for himself. (If the big backstory reveal doesn't happen here, then the second most workable place is at the end of Act Two. By then, the story should be racing toward a conclusion, so backstory may have to be pruned to a "just the facts, ma'am" few lines.)

If a trap was laid in the previous event, the fifth sequence's initiating event is where it's sprung. Or if the protagonist was trapped by the villain, this is where he escapes. Sometimes the hero knows it's a trap, but decides the risk is worth it, as in the movie *The Adventures of Robin Hood* when Robin enters Prince John's archery tournament for a chance at seeing Maid Marian again. In Vera Caspary's *Laura*, the hero attempts to trap a suspect, but is foiled by the heroine's tip off.

Often this event plunges the protagonist into great internal conflict between competing values, and most often one of those values is love.

This is when protagonists realize they're in love and what it may cost them, which raises the stakes in the External Throughline. Sometimes this conflict manifests in a love scene, which is frequently interrupted by a dose of cold reality.

Series protagonists may experience back-to-back attacks in the Cut Off and Reversal events. Because series protagonists commonly do not grow but rather strengthen their commitment to certain values, the Midpoint events are designed to test their resolve instead of pushing them to change. Thus the antagonist may attack the protagonist's morals in the Cut Off event, which the protagonist defends successfully against by relying upon a positive strength. But that same moral strength ironically makes him vulnerable for the Villain's attack against his external goal here in the Reversal event. Which tempts the protagonist to curse his good qualities for making him a fool.

Identifying Characteristics—

▸ The protagonist asks questions, looks for answers, and discovers essential information explaining why his earlier plan failed.

▸ Armed with new data, the protagonist takes stock of the antagonist's or villain's strengths and realizes what he's got to do is going to be *much* harder than he thought or planned for before.

▸ The protagonist takes inventory of his own resources and realizes fully how worse off he is now than before his half-cocked efforts.

▸ The protagonist comes face-to-face with a conflict in values (Love versus fill-in-the-blank), and is forced to re-examine what he really wants and what he's willing to do or not do to get it.

- The protagonist escapes from a trap, walks into a trap, or is foiled from springing a trap of his own.

- A major clue comes to light, but is often obscured, discounted, or set aside. (Even in non-mysteries.)

- In romances, if the Big Love Scene did *not* occur in the last event then it occurs here as an expression of the central conflict.

- In mysteries, the villain always makes an appearance at this event, but usually never as the prime suspect. For example, in Caspary's *Laura,* the detective hero sets a trap for Laura's fiance (suspect), but Waldo (killer) unexpectedly stumbles into it.

Other names for this event: Midpoint (Snyder) (Field); The Supreme Ordeal (Vogler); Turning Point #3: the Point of No Return (Hauge); The Hook: Midpoint (Mernit); Gives Up What Kept Her Stuck (Hudson); When Life Gives You Lemons... (Schechter).

EXAMPLES

The Alaskan, by James Oliver Curwood – Alan slams back down to earth when he learns how Mary politely kidnapped gold miner Stampede Smith to guide her through hell and high water to Alan's home. She's a fugitive, but from what...or whom?

Jessica's First Prayer, by Hesba Stretton – Jessica is intent on finding out answers about what a minister and God are.

Tarzan of the Apes, by Edgar Rice Burroughs – Tarzan stealthily rescues Jane's absentminded father and academic friend from a lion attack on the beach.

Fifth Sequence — Stripped Away (50% - 62.5%) — This sequence is all about consequences and fallout from the previous event. Blake Snyder called this stage "The Bad Guys Close In." The key here is to keep in mind "bad guys" could be villains or the protagonist's own belief system crashing down. "Bad guys" might even be good guys who are simply antagonistic to the protagonist's flaw and set out to make him see the light. That agenda often hands the reins of the fifth sequence to someone other than the protagonist, such as the antagonist or love interest.

The protagonist's big plan has failed disastrously, and now he is compelled to accept responsibility for his own problems. Or now's the time that stolen fruit he was snacking on so victoriously at the Midpoint turns into a mouthful of gravel. He is forced to confront his fear, wound, or flawed belief and his need to change. For example, in a romance the Cut Off event might have the hero break up with the heroine because of his jealousy over her friendship with another man. Now in this sequence he's so miserable without her he's forced to admit to himself the other man isn't what's keeping them apart, but rather his own deep-seated rigidity and insecurity. Or perhaps the Reversal event was the Big Love Scene, where the heroine risked abandoning her self-defenses to let love in. Now in the cold light of a new day she's hit square between the eyes with the reality of what she's done. She's fallen in love with the personification of her worst fears, and that truth makes her bolt like a rabbit who woke up and realized it was hunting season.

All this doesn't happen in a single scene, but in different ways throughout the sequence. The protagonist is barraged by external and internal forces tearing away his false beliefs about the way things are. It's painful to face the truth, but the Midpoint events knocked the rose-colored glasses off his face, and now no matter where he turns he's confronted by harsh reality.

Identifying Characteristics—

▸ Sometimes begins with a brief celebration, where the protagonist is off his guard. He's survived the Midpoint events, maybe even erroneously believes his plan worked. He may feel it's time to "make love, not war."

▸ The antagonist demonstrates his motivation and commitment to *his* goal and takes control of the story, driving the sequence.

▸ The antagonist regroups and attacks in force.

▸ The protagonist is on the run, if not physically, then emotionally and psychologically, as the truth of his own culpability breaths down his neck.

▸ The protagonist's support systems (beliefs, alliances, etc.) fail or are deliberately stripped away, leaving him isolated and forced to endure alone.

▸ A subplot plays out that throws the protagonist's moral choice into high relief.

▸ New supporting characters may be introduced.

Other names for this sequence: Bad Guys Close In (Snyder); Reward (Vogler); Complications and Higher Stakes (Hauge); Kingdom in Chaos (Hudson); ...Make Lemonade! (Schechter).

EXAMPLES

The Alaskan, by James Oliver Curwood – Mary wins over Alan's men, so that when Stampede finds proof she's working as John Graham's agent, he almost doesn't tell Alan. Despite the seemingly incontrovertible evidence, Alan chooses to believe in her integrity.

Jessica's First Prayer, by Hesba Stretton – Jessica prays for God to repay Daniel for his kindness, but after extracting a vow of secrecy from her in order to protect his dual incomes, Daniel privately worries about how God will reckon with him for his avarice.

Tarzan of the Apes, by Edgar Rice Burroughs – Tarzan cautiously befriends helpless members of the marooned party, one of whom is a relative of the deceased Lord and Lady Greystoke, whose remains are discovered and given proper burial. Tarzan falls in love from afar with the cultured Jane.

Sixth Sequence's Initiating Event — Hope Lost (62.5% - 65%) —

The earlier Reversal event might have seemed bad, but at least the protagonist had friends on his side then. After his physical and emotional support systems have been stripped away in the previous sequence, the protagonist is worse off now than before. He can never go back to the way things were, either because the old world has been ruined for him, or, like Eliza Doolittle in *My Fair Lady*, he's been ruined for that world. It's the Big Black Moment as he loses all hope of achieving his goal.

Physically or symbolically, something dies here. Mentors often return in this event, sometimes to bite the dust, a final blow leaving the protagonist truly alone. The training wheels on the protagonist's character arc come flying off, and he crashes face first into a brick wall that jars his entire being. The Reversal event made the protagonist consider the world in a new light, but this is the event that kills his old way of thinking once and for all.

It also calls back to the third sequence's culminating Fear Made Real event, tying into the same throughline in a way that powerfully raises the stakes again. For example, in a western at the Fear Made Real event, the newly arrived gunslinger-hero might have discovered one of his fellow stagecoach travelers was murdered and wonders if the perpetrators were after his secret stash of gold. Now at the Hope Lost event the murderers spring an ambush on him. The stakes skyrocket, because what he so greatly feared has come upon him.

Occasionally, this event is a "false victory" where success is celebrated prematurely when the finish line comes within sight, but has yet to be crossed. In this case, the protagonist alone may hold himself aloof from the festivities. He's come too far along in his character arc to ignore the threatening hardship ahead, and busies himself quietly assessing the enemy's strengths. Coming within sight of the end for him means getting another look at his worst fear, and that's nothing to make merry about.

In romances, this is where something happens to the main protagonist (either the hero or the heroine, depending upon which one has the most room to grow) that forces him to choose between love and his external goal. The choice can go either way, depending on how the conflict has been set up. If the strongest obstacle keeping the couple apart is internal (fears, wounds, flawed beliefs, etc.), then he reverts one final time to his flaw and makes the wrong choice! Fear makes him sacrifice the relationship. But if the strongest obstacle between them is external (abduction, forbidden love, fish out of water, etc.), he chooses the relationship—though without guarantees—and sacrifices his external goal, only to have that choice severely tested in the rest of the sequence as it leaves him vulnerable to a death blow delivered by the villain.

Identifying Characteristics—

- The antagonist strips away the last and most precious thing the protagonist is clinging to, leaving him totally vulnerable and at rock bottom.
- Something or someone dies, either physically, emotionally, or metaphorically. Loss, separation, isolation.

▸ A Mentor may return to die or changes sides to join the enemy.

▸ The protagonist undergoes a major viewpoint shift. He is forced to acknowledge that his old way of thinking totally let him down, and there is nothing left of it to cling to.

▸ The protagonist may experience a "false victory."

▸ The protagonist may choose to give up his goal for the sake of the love interest in the Relationship Throughline. OR...

▸ The protagonist may choose to give up the love interest in the Relationship Throughline for the sake of his goal.

Other names for this event: All is Lost (Snyder); Pinch Point #2 (Fields); Inside the Whale (Schechter); "Christ On the Cross"; Belly of the Beast; Inside the Darkest Cave; the Big Black Moment.

EXAMPLES

The Alaskan, by James Oliver Curwood – Knowing Alan loves her, Mary offers to explain everything, warning him that the truth about her and John Graham is worse than any of his darkest suspicions.

Jessica's First Prayer, by Hesba Stretton – The minister visits Jessica where she lives in a miserable loft above a stable, but is unable to help her.

Tarzan of the Apes, by Edgar Rice Burroughs – Just as Tarzan prepares to declare his love for her, Jane is kidnapped by the exiled ape, Terkoz, who is bent on revenge. While her loved ones abandon all hope, Tarzan gives pursuit and rescues her.

Sixth Sequence — Win or Lose (62.5% - 75%) — The final sequence of Act Two charts the emotional aftermath of the Hope Lost event. The thing the protagonist most hoped for has died, and now realization begins to dawn with a new hope. A new understanding. The positive side of the theme takes root in his heart.

Earlier, in the Breakthrough sequence, the antagonist's plans were explained to the protagonist, inspiring false confidence in his ability to deal with the problem. At the Cut Off and Reversal events, those plans turned out to be phony, incomplete, or only half-true. Now the complete picture of the antagonist's designs are laid out before the protagonist, and they are infinitely worse than his worst nightmares. If the protagonist was already down and out from the Hope Lost event, the sense arrives here that the antagonist is closing in for the kill.

This revelation comes as a direct result of the protagonist's goals shifting at the Hope Lost event. Usually it comes because he takes a step back from the problem that has obsessed him for the whole story. He was too close to it before, pushing too hard. Now he gains a new comprehension of the composition and magnitude of the antagonist's plans.

The physical and emotional stakes of the story are again established, setting the stage for Act Three. But right now, the protagonist has no idea how to save the day. There is no false pride left. He's defeated, and there is no more obfuscation about his ownership of this hopeless situation. Enemy or no, the protagonist's own flaw is the greater to blame. He knows it, and accepts it. He's learned his lesson, though it has yet to be proven in Act Three whether he will stick by it.

The protagonist is finally ready to change his focus, his hierarchy of values. He makes a new plan and puts it into action. This time his plan isn't so much about winning as mere survival. He makes a desperate attempt to recover or regroup the alliances and relationships that were recently stripped away from him. For a brief time it seems as though he has a chance, however tenuous. But even if he seems to succeed, it's a success that exists only so long as the protagonist can keep it hidden under the antagonist's radar.

Identifying Characteristics—

▸ The protagonist confesses the truth about his motivations, and his fear, wound, or flawed belief is plainly revealed. Often in public and to humiliating effect.

▸ The theme is restated, by the protagonist this time, showing he's accepted it for himself.

▸ The antagonist's *real* plans are explained to or by the protagonist. This time what he only partially understood before becomes wholly and horribly clear.

▸ Allies debate the protagonist's chances of survival. They aren't good.

▸ If the protagonist gave up his goal for love at the Hope Lost event, now he discovers he's lost love, too. OR...

▸ If the protagonist gave up love for his goal at the Hope Lost event, now he discovers his goal doesn't satisfy him like he expected. It's empty.

▸ The protagonist implements a new plan, informed by a change in values, to recover what was lost and hide out, sometimes under the antagonist's very nose.

Other names for this sequence: the Dark Night of the Soul (Snyder); Reward - continued (Vogler); Death and Rebirth (Schechter).

EXAMPLES

The Alaskan, by James Oliver Curwood – Mary is the runaway bride of John Graham, the man who viciously ruined and murdered Alan's father. Their love forbidden, Alan rides the range alone, planning to return stateside with her to confront their enemy together.

Jessica's First Prayer, by Hesba Stretton – Jessica keeps Daniel's secret from the minister, who provides the child with enough money for daily breakfasts at the coffee-stall.

Tarzan of the Apes, by Edgar Rice Burroughs – Sheltered by the jungle, Tarzan and Jane's innocent love flourishes until civilization closes in on them in the form of a French naval rescue party. When the French fall into the clutches of cannibals, Tarzan leaves Jane to rescue them.

Act Three

Seventh Sequence's Initiating Event — New Direction (75% - 77.5%) — The antagonist catches on to the protagonist's plan with devastating consequences. This event flicks on the light bulb over the protagonist's head. The solution to all his problems is unified in one idea. While the event is spurred by the antagonist, often the idea is delivered directly or indirectly by the love interest in the Relationship Throughline, because that throughline most clearly demonstrates the protagonist's character growth. This relationship is a source of strength to the protagonist, energizing him to recommit to his goal against all odds. But this is not the same old cumbersome goal he's pursued from the beginning. This new incarnation of his goal is shaped and informed by his character growth and the positive aspects of the theme.

Whether or not he discovers he has anything left to lose in a contest with the antagonist, the power of the protagonist's motivation resides now with the love interest. If he fails to make the attempt, the love interest will in some way suffer severe loss. The threatened loss may be physical or emotional. Regardless, the protagonist is willing to go down trying rather than let the love interest suffer. His is a decision recast in the mold of sacrificial courage.

In stories other than romances, the love interest doesn't even necessarily have to be alive to exert this magical influence upon the protagonist's decision. It could be a beloved mentor who has passed away earlier, but whose investment of faith in the protagonist hangs in jeopardy.

Despite the influences around him, the protagonist makes this decision on his own. No one tricks or cajoles him, or makes it for him. He makes it with clear intent and purpose, with no guarantee of success and every chance of devastating defeat.

Identifying Characteristics—

▸ The protagonist's plan to survive and hide nearly destroys him.
▸ The antagonist sweeps in for the killing blow.
▸ The love interest in the Relationship Throughline directly or indirectly inspires the protagonist to recommit to a nobler version of his goal.
▸ The love interest is threatened with loss.
▸ The protagonist intentionally commits of his own free will.

Other names for this event: Break Into Three (Snyder); The Road Back (Vogler); Turning Point #4: the Major Setback (Hauge); Swivel: Second Turning Point (Mernit); Plot Point #2 (Field); Wanders in the Wilderness (Hudson); What's the Worst That Can Happen? (Schechter).

EXAMPLES

The Alaskan, by James Oliver Curwood – Far away on the tundra, Stampede delivers a life-and-death message from Mary urgently summoning Alan back home. Upon his return, he finds Mary trapped, Rossland in his cabin, and John Graham on the way.

Jessica's First Prayer, by Hesba Stretton – Jessica fails to show up for Sunday services or for breakfast with Daniel two weeks in a row.

Tarzan of the Apes, by Edgar Rice Burroughs – The captured French are given up for dead. Jane's jealous suitor accuses her missing forest god of conspiring with the cannibals, unaware that Tarzan has taken a surviving officer into his care.

Seventh Sequence — **Final Push (75% - 87.5%)** — The protagonist formulates a new plan to win, gain, or achieve his new goal, and puts the plan into action. A key component of his plan involves confronting his fear, wound, or flawed belief. Like Rick in *Casablanca*, whose wound taught him to stick his neck out for no one, that's exactly what's involved in getting Ilsa and her husband safely out of the country. Total commitment to his new and nobler goal tolerates no half-hearted effort. The protagonist must face his fear head-on, expecting and even daring the worst to happen. He throws in his lot with the theme, trusting against all odds that this time his efforts will turn out victorious.

This sequence in many ways echoes a more intense version of the Breakthrough sequence that led up to the Cut Off event. The protagonist gathers allies back around him to help put his plan into action, and charges forward toward the antagonist. These allies are usually different than those he started out with on his journey. They may have acted antagonistic toward his flaw before, trying to make him see the light, and now he has work to do convincing them to join up with him. They may insist he prove whether he can be trusted. Or they may be old allies he alienated with his flaw and now he must humble himself to earn their assistance and renewed friendship. The daredevil, against-all-odds nature of the plan probably goes a long way toward convincing them of his sincerity. Either way, there isn't a whole lot of time to spend getting reacquainted, as there's time pressure involved.

The time pressure could be a deadline, with the protagonist racing against the clock. It might be an escape, where it's only a matter of time before they're detected or their means of rescue is closed off. It could be a chase, with either the protagonist chasing the antagonist, or the antagonist chasing the protagonist. In romances, the protagonist may literally chase after the love interest to prove he's worthy of another chance at happily-ever-after or save her from the villain.

Identifying Characteristics—

▸ Protagonist comes up with a new plan to achieve his goal.

▸ The protagonist's plan depends upon his challenging his fear, wound or flawed belief head-on, thus inviting his worst nightmare.

▸ There are no guarantees or hope of personal reward.

▸ Protagonist recruits and gathers new allies to his side.

▸ Some allies may die or suffer debilitating defeat for having signed on to the protagonist's plan, thus reemphasizing the stakes and testing the strength of his commitment.

▸ Often a chase, escape, or race against time commences.

▸ Early success breathes to life a faint hope that the protagonist's plan might actually work.

Other names for this sequence: Gathering the Team / Executing the Plan (Snyder); The Final Push (Hauge).

EXAMPLES

The Alaskan, by James Oliver Curwood – Rossland reveals Graham's plan to buy Alan's silence in exchange for isolation to rape, imprison, and murder Mary. Alan drives Rossland out, and the lovers prepare to flee to Nome.

Jessica's First Prayer, by Hesba Stretton – Daniel's anxiety for Jessica overcomes his fear of discovery, and he risks enlisting the minister's assistance to locate the child. Finding her deathly ill, he repents for loving money more than people.

Tarzan of the Apes, by Edgar Rice Burroughs – Tarzan faithfully tends Lieutenant D'Arnot's severe wounds, though caring for his new friend delays his yearned for return to Jane. She waits, but is finally compelled to leave Africa–and her forest lover–behind.

Eighth Sequence's Initiating Event — Sacrifice (87.5% - 90%) — The faint spark of hope ignited toward the end of the previous sequence sets up the protagonist for his biggest fall ever. His harebrained scheme seemed to be working, when suddenly the antagonist yanks the rug out from under him. His success merely positioned him for the antagonist to spring a trap, and he is brought to his knees. His plan is finished. There's nothing left he can do. The very worst of the worst has befallen him, only it's infinitely harder to endure than any nightmare, because the one person in the world who means the most to him (the love interest) will suffer because of his failure.

Here is where the protagonist's commitment to his new and nobler purpose is put to the ultimate test. Before, he tried his flawed way of doing things but it didn't work. Then he tried the nobler way of doing things, and now it has failed, too. It looks like there's no winning whichever path he tries, and the message of the theme seems a colossal cosmic joke at his expense. The protagonist learns the hard way that his faith in the theme was merely intellectual assent, and works without faith is suicide. Not only has the antagonist won, but his victory includes grinding the protagonist's newly adopted belief system into dust and ashes. This is his Job 13:15 moment, when the reader holds her breath, wondering if he will curse the truth of the theme and die—or instead grit out, "Though the theme slay me, yet will I trust in it."

This event plays out in one of two ways, as either a sacrifice or confrontation. If it's a sacrifice, then the thing sacrificed represents in some tangible way the character's flawed goal. He gives it up without any possible chance for reward or saving grace, simply because he's learned the thematic lesson and now knows it's the right thing to do. As in J.R.R. Tolkien's *The Hobbit*, when Bilbo sacrifices the fabulous Arkenstone diamond, which is the supreme prize of the treasure they spent the whole story questing after, to save the dwarves from war. He still has a claim to a portion of the remaining treasure, but no guarantee of receiving any. He's still going back to his friends, but it's almost certain the dwarves will reject him for what they'll perceive as a "betrayal."

If it's a confrontation between the protagonist and antagonist, the "battle" results in defeat for the protagonist. As in Suzanne Collins' *The Hunger Games*, when Katniss and Peeta head toward the final showdown with the last tribute opposing them, Cato. Except when they encounter him, they discover the living are outnumbered by the dead tributes who have been turned into muttations and trap them atop the burning hot cornucopia. Cato captures the injured Peeta, choking him to death, and Katniss knows she's going to lose him and then Cato will kill her. Sometimes the confrontation is not physical, so much as emotional. As in the movie, *While You Were Sleeping*, when Jack brings Lucy the Florence snow globe as a wedding present, and she asks him if he can give her any reason not to marry his brother. "I can't," he says, and leaves. It's her big defeat, the moment when she believes the man she truly loves doesn't want her.

Which is why this confrontation has to occur between the protagonist and antagonist, not their proxies. No one else can step in to "take one for the team." And no Mentor need come along now to help out, either. The protagonist is totally on his own. Everything rests on his shoulders, and the awesome responsibility of it is intense pressure.

Identifying Characteristics—

- The "ticking clock" counts down to the final seconds, and the alarm goes off!
- The protagonist and antagonist come face-to-face in a final confrontation.
- The antagonist springs a trap!
- Sometimes a surprise connection is revealed between two characters which tests loyalties and shifts the balance of power.
- The kiss of Judas! A trusted ally may be revealed a traitor, either willingly or under compulsion.
- A character believed dead may be revealed to be alive.
- There's nothing left for the protagonist to try. His plan is over and done.
- The protagonist has one final opportunity to reject his recent internal change and revert to a worst flawed state than he began.

Other names for this event: The High Tower Surprise (Snyder); Resurrection (Vogler); Turning Point #5: the Climax (Hauge); The Dark Moment: Crisis Climax (Mernit); Climax (Field); Chooses Her Light (Hudson); Good Guy Versus Bad Guy Over Stakes (Schechter).

> EXAMPLES
>
> *The Alaskan*, by James Oliver Curwood – John Graham's private army arrives and turns Alan's cabin into a deathtrap. Mary pleads with him to give her up to save himself, but he gladly accepts the loss of everything including life itself to protect her.
>
> *Jessica's First Prayer*, by Hesba Stretton – Daniel abandons the coffee-stall to nurse Jessica in his own home and sends a message summoning the minister to the dying child's bedside. His heart turns to God, and he repents of his sins.
>
> *Tarzan of the Apes*, by Edgar Rice Burroughs – Tarzan sacrifices his jungle life to search for Jane and return D'Arnot to civilization, where his soul chafes even as he becomes a fine gentleman.

Eighth Sequence — Do or Die (87.5% - 100%) — The protagonist realizes the only thing left for him to do is the one thing he swore he would never do. For Rick in *Casablanca*, whose wound was being left in the rain at a Parisian train station, it's deliberately being abandoned. Again. By the same woman who broke his heart before. It's Aragorn in *The Lord of the Rings: The Return of the King* marching out as the leader of Gondor's allied forces to face Sauron in battle, purely on faith that his sacrifice will give Frodo the opportunity to succeed. He has no hope of duking it out successfully with the Lord of Mordor's armies, and it's the last thing Sauron expects precisely because it's the one thing everyone has tried so hard to avoid.

This is how stories come full circle to tie the backstory and present story together satisfactorily. Not only does the protagonist have the opportunity to relive the greatest wound from his past, but he *chooses* to do so in order to redeem the present. Inspired by a prize greater than any he coveted for himself, the protagonist gives the last full measure. He steps out by faith wholly into the theme's embrace without any kind of safety net. Deadly pain seems the only certain outcome of his plan.

If the Sacrifice event saw the protagonist make an actual sacrifice, then the resulting confrontation between protagonist and antagonist is left to play out here. As in *The Hobbit*, when Bilbo returns to the mountain fortress and owns up to Thorin about "burgling" the Arkenstone to negotiate peace and their survival. Thorin attacks him and is barely restrained from killing Bilbo in a fit of rage. Instead he throws Bilbo out of the fortress.

On the other hand, if the Sacrifice event launched this final sequence with the main confrontation between protagonist and antagonist, then it remains for the protagonist to make that big sacrifice here. The protagonist came out of the confrontation defeated. He has no expectation of selfish gain by giving up what he held most dear, except that it's the right thing to do. As in the movie *While You Were Sleeping*, when Lucy objects at her own wedding and confesses to the family she was never engaged to Peter, and is in fact in love with Jack (which she believes is unrequited). Or in *The Hunger Games*, when the Gamekeepers revoke the rules permitting two winners to live. Rather than fight each other to the death and live with the horrible consequences, Katniss and Peeta risk sacrificing their lives in a mutual suicide pact.

Of course, it's the protagonist's genuine faith in the theme, even to his own certain ruin, that overcomes the antagonist and saves the day. His plan finally succeeds! The love interest is vindicated or delivered from whatever threat the antagonist held over her. The protagonist is recognized for his inherent value, worth, and personal authority. His world is put back together, but changed and better than before.

In a mystery, here's where all the lose ends are tied up and explained. Or in a romance, the lovers embrace for their happily ever after, perhaps even indulging in an epilogue with a wedding or a new addition to the family.

Identifying Characteristics—

▸ The protagonist sacrifices something vitally important.

▸ The protagonist takes a leap of faith.

▸ The protagonist does something he would have *never* done voluntarily before.

▸ The protagonist does something the antagonist never anticipated.

▸ The protagonist chooses to relive a painful wound from his past or deliberately make his greatest fear come true.

▸ The protagonist's plan succeeds, and he conquers the antagonist to win, gain, or achieve what he values more than himself (often personified in some way by the love interest).

▸ There's a little extra, unexpected reward for the protagonist. He doesn't see this one coming—it's a complete surprise. He is offered or given a "healthier" version of what he wanted at the beginning.

▸ May wrap up with a snapshot of the protagonist's new life where his relationships are healed and community restored.

Other names for this sequence: Dig Deep Down / Execution of the New Plan (Snyder); Return with the Elixir (Vogler); the Aftermath

(Hauge); Joyful Defeat: Resolution (Mernit); Re-ordering / Rescue / The Kingdom is Brighter (Hudson).

EXAMPLES

The Alaskan, by James Oliver Curwood – Alan sends Mary out through a secret trapdoor and remains behind as decoy for their enemies, sacrificing himself in a bid to buy her time to escape. She returns for him, and together they flee ahead of Graham's men into a ravine where Alan's shot and she's captured. Stampede arrives with Alan's men in time to dispatch Graham, and the lovers, now free, prepare to wed.

Jessica's First Prayer, by Hesba Stretton – Daniel would rather give away every penny he's earned than lose the child, and confesses his double life to the minister. Seeing how much she means to Daniel, Jessica prays and is restored to a healthy, happy life as his foster daughter.

Tarzan of the Apes, by Edgar Rice Burroughs – Awaiting evidence that he's the son and true heir of Lord Greystoke, Tarzan locates Jane and saves her from a forest fire, but too late to save her from choosing security over love. Brokenhearted, he denies his aristocratic birth and returns to the African jungle.

(The above examples are provided in a unified format in the Appendixes at the back of this book. For *The Alaskan*, please refer to Appendix A. *Jessica's First Prayer* can be found in Appendix B. And *Tarzan of the Apes* is Appendix C.)

These eight sequences with the culminating or initiating events are the connecting bones and joints that form a story's skeleton. They are the same in function the world over, but unique in design every time. They are listed above in a manner emphasizing an upbeat outcome, where the protagonist learns the lesson of the theme and ultimately prevails over his problem. If X-raying a tragedy or cautionary tale (favored by some horror or literary fiction), a general rule of thumb is to follow the antagonist's journey instead of the protagonist's. From this altered perspective, high points become lows and low points become highs.

Premise and Archetypes

Reader interest hinges on drama, and drama is born of conflict. Man versus man. Man versus nature. Man versus self. Protagonist and antagonist motivated by opposing values. And where do those universal values come from?

Theme. Or, more precisely, *thematic conflict*. Because theme is really a battle royal between weakness and strength, vice and virtue, good and evil. It is, in short, a moral conflict. A moral conflict is about right and wrong, and forces the characters to make sacrificial choices that test the inner principles they live by.

Stories fall off the cliff into preachiness when writers mistake social issues for moral issues. Social issues are defined by cultures and society, and go in and out of awareness with the times. They are what society deems important right now, and appreciable change can only be recognized when large groups of people shift positions. For example, "global warming" is a social issue unknown in public awareness until recently. Achieving dramatic change in a story about it would necessarily involve a large group of people, thus dispersing and depersonalizing the conflict.

Moral issues are both timeless and personal. Who, throughout human history, has not been challenged by issues of love, hope, honor, envy, fear, jealousy, etc.? They are the beat of the human heart, and the true motivation for the kind of individual change that eventually ripples outward into a family, a community, and society. For example, a thematic conflict that essentially states "cruelty to animals is bad" says nothing about the internal motivations that drive some people to harm animals and others to risk their lives to protect animals.

The most effective place for social issues in stories is as a stage for the moral conflict to play out. For example, "a young orphan discovers unconditional love while trying to heal an abused horse." In this scenario, the issue of animal cruelty provides the backdrop for the moral theme of unconditional love leading to redemption. By the end, animal cruelty will still exist in the society of the story world, but dramatically appreciable change will have occurred in the protagonist and her horse.

The Three-Act Structure naturally supports the development of theme. Whether a writer is working with a closed theme (a statement) or an open theme (a question), it usually can be broken down into three parts.

EXAMPLE
Unconditional love / leads to / redemption.
Can unconditional love / lead to / redemption?

Stanley D. Williams, author of *The Moral Premise* book and his similarly titled writing blog, expands the classic thematic statement into a premise statement containing negative and positive values. He calls these two extremes *vices* and *virtues.* The protagonist starts out the story hampered by a vice, and travels toward a saving virtue. The irony is that the vice and virtue are often polar opposites of each other, so the protagonist's challenge is to achieve a healthy balance.

It's this conflict of values that informs every act, every scene, and every exchange of dialogue. They motivate characters to drive the story by taking dramatically meaningful actions. They're the best reason for the existence of subplots and supporting characters.

So what does a moral premise look like? It's a pair of negative and positive thematic statements, wherein psychological values lead to specific physical states. Psychological values are behaviors that impact others. Physical states are material realities that impact the acting character. In other words, specific choices result in specific consequences.

EXAMPLE
Deception leads to injustice and persecution, but
Honesty leads to justice and freedom.

Pretty simple on the surface. Stimulus and response. Cause and effect. But it's simple premises like this that layer three-dimensional flesh on the bones of dramatic story structure.

Act One
Protagonist doesn't want to give up his vice, and even rejects the moral premise outright.

Act Two (first half)
Protagonist decides to try the negative extreme of the moral premise and fails before finally accepting the truth.

Act Two (second half)
Protagonist tries the positive side of the moral premise, and winds up burning all his bridges in an all-or-nothing gamble.

Act Three
Protagonist faces a "fight to the death" where his commitment to the moral premise is proven and he's victorious.

If a villain personifies the negative side of the moral premise, then usually his storyline ends in tragedy. He represents the "but for the grace of God go I" consequences of stubbornly rejecting the moral premise. But if the story has an antagonist who actually tries to help the protagonist grow and change into a better person, such as in romance novels, then the antagonist achieves a healthy thematic balance that complements the protagonist's arc. The love interest typically represents the thematic value the protagonist unconsciously wishes he could embrace, if only he dared. Together they achieve harmony.

The best stories cast each and every character in thematically significant roles. The villain does more than mess with the protagonist and give him a bad day. He personifies the antithesis of the theme. A best friend isn't there just to have coffee with the heroine and listen to her pour out her troubles. The best friend provides a unique attitude and perspective on the theme, too. Each character acts like a funhouse mirror, reflecting the truth of the theme back at the protagonist and the reader in a new and different way.

There are eight such thematic roles that can appear in a story, regardless of genre. Some of these archetypes may suggest certain personality types (and a few even share similar-sounding labels), but these archetypes differ from personality types for significant reasons.

Personality types, because they characterize a person's dominant thought and behavior patterns, do not change mid-story. The character may become healthier or unhealthier in the expression of his thoughts and behaviors, but his bedrock motivations remain constant. For example, a person who is focused on power and control may want to use it to protect the weak (healthy expression) or bully and intimidate others (unhealthy expression), but either way his fixation is the same.

Thematic archetypes, on the other hand, are all about fulfilling a *role* in the story, and that role can change at any time. They serve the dramatic function of reflecting various angles of the thematic conflict, and have no direct link with personality types. For example, in director Christopher Nolan's film, *Batman Begins*, Ducard begins the story in the role of Bruce Wayne's mentor, but by the end his role metamorphoses into Batman's antagonist. However, Ducard's personality remains consistent.

The one exception to shifting archetypal roles is that of the protagonist, whose thematic presence on the page should remain singularly focused. Not all eight roles appear in every story, but the first four are crucial.

The Protagonist — The character who changes the most, drives the decisions at major turning points, and makes the greatest sacrifice at the end.

The Antagonist — The thematic opposite of the protagonist. The character who directly challenges the protagonist's flawed beliefs.

The Mentor — The thematic protector of the protagonist's moral center, that part of the character that is essentially good and heroic. Offers help and advice.

The Deflector — (Sometimes called the Contagonist.) The character who challenges the protagonist to try a different way of doing things. In romances, this role is often combined with antagonist and personified in the love interest.

The Sidekick — (Sometimes called the Ally or Believer.) The character who loyally supports the protagonist's way of doing things, just as they are, without any changes.

The Skeptic — (Sometimes called the Doubter.) The character who represents the audience's disbelief, addresses it from within the story, and allows the reader to accept what's happening. (Example: Joan Wilder's editor in *Romancing the Stone* warns, "Joan, you're not up to this.")

The Thinker — (Sometimes called the Logic character.) The character who represents the intellectual side of the thematic argument, a wait-and-see approach.

The Feeler — (Sometimes called the Emotion character.) The character who represents the emotional side of the thematic argument, personified in chaotic, impulsive behavior.

For more insight into thematic roles and detailed examples of how they work together in various types of stories, I highly recommend Jeffrey Alan Schechter's fun book, *My Story Can Beat Up Your Story!*

Character Growth

Character growth is the lifeblood of stories. The protagonist may go through hell and high water, but that's not enough to satisfy a reader. A story only feels worth the reading if the character grows and changes. It's the protagonist's growth that is largely responsible for individualizing universal structure patterns into unique stories.

There are three basic ways a character can change during the course of a story. Each way, when applied to the classic structure described earlier, makes the story look different. When examining book X-rays, it's helpful to understand these three different character paths (also called "arcs") to avoid confusion and cultivate inspiration.

In *The Inner Game of Screenwriting,* Sandy Frank explores the three basic character arcs most commonly used. He also details hybrids and alterations, but they all boil down to these three:

1. The character begins with a flaw that's eroding his happiness, and because of the conflict encountered in pursuit of an external goal, changes into a better person. This is by far the most popular character arc for protagonists to make, and the one most likely to resonate with readers of genre fiction.

2. A character begins as a healthy person, but because of the conflict encountered in pursuit of an external goal, his values are refined by his fiery trials and he becomes even stronger. (Think of any John Wayne movie or long-running fiction series with a recurring central protagonist, like Earl Stanley Gardner's Perry Mason.)

3. A character begins as a seemingly healthy person, but because of the conflict encountered in pursuit of an external goal, his values are compromised and weakened until he's worse off than at the beginning. This one shows up a lot in literary fiction.

The same story structure "bones" come alive in totally different ways when energized by these three styles of character arcs.

In the first scenario, Act 1 shows how the character's flaw is eroding his happiness, while the events and sequences in Act 2 push him to be a better person, until Act 3 shows the finished product of his internal change.

The second scenario shapes itself differently. Act 1 shows how the character's values make things harder for him, while the conflicts in Act 2 do everything to push him off track and into betraying those values, until Act 3 shows him rising from the ashes hardened like steel in his convictions.

The third scenario belongs to tragedies and cautionary tales like Mario Puzo's *The Godfather* and F. Scott Fitzgerald's *The Great Gatsby*. Act 1 demonstrates the character's values, while Act 2 tempts and pressures him into compromising his very soul, until in Act 3 he's a moral shadow of the person he once was.

If the character's growth arc is the lifeblood of the tale, then the character's personality is the unique DNA swirling through the blood. It informs which flaws are convincing fits for which characters.

The Enneagram is an ancient personality system that defines nine levels of psychological health for each of nine different personality types (which can be further broken down into hundreds of variations). No personality type is good or bad, but they can be emotionally healthy or unhealthy in their attitudes and behaviors. Hence, the Enneagram is a great way to pin down a character's motivations and shape his growth. The flaw or vice that the protagonist begins the story with is an unhealthy expression of his personality type, while the virtue the protagonist grows toward is a healthy expression of his personality type.

One word of warning, though. If a person is at the lowest, most unhealthy level imaginable, it's highly unlikely he can change enough to reach the highest level of health. So unlikely, as a matter of fact, as to be utterly in the realm of Divine Intervention. So unless a character experiences a Saul-on-the-road-to-Damascus miracle, most character arcs are going to play out somewhere in the middle and span only two or three health levels at most.

Here is a list of one-word characteristics (both positive and negative) associated with each of the nine Enneagram types, compiled from the excellent book *Personality Types: Using the Enneagram for Self-Discovery* (1996), by Don Richard Riso with Russ Hudson. The words are arranged in order from Healthy to Unhealthy. The nine types are arranged in numerical order with descriptive names to help differentiate them. Famous fictional characters associated with each type are also listed for reference.

Type One - Perfectionist

Wise, reasonable, responsible, striving, orderly, critical, inflexible, contradictory, punishing.

Examples in stories: Atticus Finch in Harper Lee's *To Kill a Mockingbird*. Elinor Dashwood in Jane Austen's *Sense and Sensibility*. Eugenia Wraxton in Georgette Heyer's *The Grand Sophy*. Javert in Victor Hugo's *Les Miserables*. Laura Holt in the TV series *Remington Steele*. Marilla Cuthbert in Lucy Maud Montgomery's *Anne of Green Gables*. Rose in *The African Queen*.

Type Two - Helper

Unconditionally loving, caring, giving, demonstrative, intrusive, overbearing, manipulative, coercive, parasitic.

Examples in stories: Addison Goodheart in Dean Koontz's *Innocence*. Annie in Stephen King's *Misery*. Belle in the TV series *Once Upon a Time*. Jack in Lisa Kleypas's *Smooth Talking Stranger*. Mr. John Jarndyce in Charles Dickens' *Bleak House*. King Lear in William Shakespeare's play by the same name. Michael Westen in the TV series *Burn Notice*. The first-person protagonist in Daphne du Maurier's *Rebecca*. Scout in Harper Lee's *To Kill a Mockingbird*. Sophy Stanton-Lacy in Georgette Heyer's *The Grand Sophy*. Dr. John Watson in Sir Arthur Conan Doyle's Sherlock Holmes stories. Dr. Wilson in the TV series *House*.

Type Three - Achiever

Authentic, admirable, self-improving, performing, expedient, self-promoting, deceptive, opportunistic, relentless.

Examples in stories: Audrey fforbes-Hamilton in the TV series *To the Manor Born*. Becky Sharp in William Makepeace Thackeray's *Vanity Fair*. Tom Sawyer in Mark Twain's *The Adventures of Tom Sawyer*. Scarlett O'Hara in Margaret Mitchell's *Gone With the Wind*.

Type Four - Individualist

Inspired, sensitive, creative, individualistic, temperamental, demanding, alienated, depressed, suicidal.

Examples in stories: Anne Shirley in Lucy Maud Montgomery's *Anne of Green Gables*. Camille in Alexandre Dumas's *Camille*. Jake Green in the TV series *Jericho*. Lucy in the movie *While You Were Sleeping*. Marianne in Jane Austen's *Sense and Sensibility*. Heathcliff in Emily Bronte's *Wuthering Heights*.

Type Five - Thinker

Visionary, perceptive, innovative, knowledgable, preoccupied, contentious, eccentric, hallucinating, psychotic.

Examples in stories: Ebenezer Scrooge in Charles Dickens's *A Christmas Carol*. Hannibal Lecter in Thomas Harris's *The Silence of the Lambs*. The title character in the TV series *House*. Sherlock Holmes in Laurie R. King's *The Beekeeper's Apprentice* and original Sir Arthur Conan Doyle stories.

Type Six - Loyalist

Courageous, reliable, cooperative, loyal, defensive, blaming, cowardly, irrational, self-destructive.

Examples in stories: Amy Fleming in the TV series *Heartland*. Captain Queeg in Herman Wouk's *The Caine Mutiny*. The Cowardly Lion in L. Frank Baum's *The Wizard of Oz*. Ella in Lisa Kleypas's *Smooth Talking Stranger*. Kate in William Shakespeare's *The Taming of the Shrew*. Madeline Westen in the TV series *Burn Notice*. The title character in the TV series *Monk*. Rumplestiltskin (aka Mr. Gold) in the TV series *Once Upon a Time*.

Type Seven - Optimist

Content, free-spirited, practical, occupied, superficial, excessive, escaping, reckless, debilitated.

Examples in stories: Auntie Mame in Patrick Dennis's *Auntie Mame*. Charles Haslemere in the TV series *The Duchess of Duke Street*. Huckleberry Finn in Mark Twain's *The Adventures of Huckleberry Finn*. Peter Pan in J.M. Barrie's *Peter Pan*. Sam Axe in the TV series *Burn Notice*. The title character in the TV series *Remington Steele*. Thomas Magnum in the TV series *Magnum, P.I.*

Type Eight - Boss

Heroic, strong, leading, hardworking, dominating, threatening, violent, terrorizing, monstrous.

Examples in stories: Charles Rivenhall in Georgette Heyer's *The Grand Sophy*. Claire McLeod in the TV series *McLeod's Daughters*. Emma Snow in the TV series *Once Upon a Time*. Fiona Glenanne in the TV series *Burn Notice*. Jean Valjean in Victor Hugo's *Les Miserables*. Katniss in Suzanne Collins' *The Hunger Games*. Louisa Trotter in the TV series *The Duchess of Duke Street*. Mary Russell in Laurie R. King's *The Beekeeper's Apprentice*. Petruchio in William Shakespeare's *The Taming of the Shrew*. Sydney Bristow in the TV series *Alias*.

Type Nine - Peacemaker

Indomitable, steady, supportive, agreeable, complacent, stubborn, neglectful, helpless, catatonic.

Examples in stories: Bilbo Baggins in J.R.R. Tolkien's *The Hobbit*. Britt Ponset in the classic radio series *The Six Shooter*. Charlie in the *The African Queen*. Matthew Cuthbert in Lucy Maud Montgomery's *Anne of Green Gables*. Mitchell Rafferty in Dean Koontz's *The Husband*. The title character in Ernest Hemingway's *The Old Man and the Sea*. Peeta in Suzanne Collins' *The Hunger Games*.

Riso and Hudson's website, www.enneagraminstitute.com, has free overviews of each type, complete with associated fears, desires, motivations, and health levels (click on "Type Descriptions"). Their book is packed from cover to cover with detailed chapters on each personality type, and is a highly recommended resource for further study. Enneagram coach Katherine Fauvre's website, enneagram.net, also offers overviews of the types, including vices, virtues, and growth paths (plus fun collages, too). Judith Searle's book, *The Literary Enneagram: Characters from the Inside Out,* is a wonderful and unique resource packed with examples of famous fictional characters. And romance author Laurie Schnebly demonstrates how each type would react in a variety of genre situations in her book *Believable Characters: Creating with Enneagrams.*

Reader Empathy and Identification

Not all protagonists are likable, prime candidates for best friend status. Some are downright curmudgeonly. A few are even cold, mean, and heartless. It doesn't really matter if the protagonist makes Pollyanna look like a miser, or Ebenezer Scrooge seem like a kitten by comparison. Likability is negotiable. Empathy is vital.

Empathy goes beyond the reader understanding what makes a character tick. Empathy is also about stimulating feelings in the reader, both feelings *for* the character, and feelings *shared* with the character. It bypasses the reader's objective intellect and grabs hold of their emotions. It begins on the first page, and compounds on every page thereafter. Because, quite simply, without it the reader will put the book down regardless of how intricate the plot or profound the theme or three-dimensional the characterization.

Empathy exists separate from reader interest. A reader can be genuinely interested in a story, yet loathe spending time with the characters. Like a really annoying neighbor, a realistic and well-developed character who nevertheless lacks essential empathetic qualities is still perfectly capable of sending a reader running for the nearest hills.

A reader might force themselves to finish the book anyway, because of an overwhelming intellectual investment in the subject, or a commitment to their book club. But without empathy, reader engagement becomes a hard chore instead of a lose-all-sense-of-time delight.

There are several things that work together in various combinations to guarantee reader empathy for a character. Some are characteristics or values belonging to the protagonist. Others are circumstances he finds himself in.

The character is a nice person — Traditional "save the cat" moments work for a reason, because people who help others, especially the less fortunate or vulnerable like animals and children, make us feel safe to be around them. This works in reverse, too, when children and animals naturally like the character. Just like a resume, the love of family, friends, or even neighbors who consider the protagonist important to them is a great recommendation to readers. While even nice characters can get mad or make mistakes, the ability to experience a change of heart or forgive wrongs returns them to center. Genuinely nice people nurture relationships and demonstrate inner values like loyalty, responsibility, and compassion even when the spotlights are turned off and no one's looking. They might even courageously risk their lives fighting for someone else or a cause they believe makes a difference in the world.

The character is in jeopardy — This could be the immediate physical danger of being injured in an accident, attacked, beaten, abused, or exploited. It could also be the longterm jeopardy of suffering a handicap, deformity, phobia, physical paralysis, addiction, disease, or financial hardship. Readers feel keenly the emotional jeopardy of losing something or someone important, either to death, abandonment, or sad circumstances. The longterm emotional jeopardy of a character haunted by his past, a wound, or any repressed pain fascinates readers who want to know how he escapes.

The character is naturally funny — Even in darkly serious stories, a character who can laugh at himself is invariably appealing. It's a sign of psychological wellbeing to have a healthy sense of humor. Enthusiasm is contagious, and readers enjoy spending time with characters whose playful, childlike innocence offers a fresh perspective on life.

The character is skilled — Whether the character enjoys all the perks of a glamorous profession or struggles against the odds in pursuit of his passion, readers are fascinated by a character who does something well. Powerful leaders exude the kind of charisma that rivet readers' attention in fiction and real life alike. Whether it's the athleticism demonstrated in sports or the hard work and persistence of a stay-at-home mom, characters who demonstrate expertise at what they do are characters clever enough to keep readers glued to the page.

The character is the victim of injustice — The classic appeal of the underdog is found in characters who suffer prejudice, unfair injury, or undeserved mistreatment. It's even more powerful if they're deceived, betrayed, or falsely accused. Perhaps they tell the truth, but no one will believe them. They know firsthand the stings and arrows of exclusion, humiliation, and embarrassment. The rejection of unrequited love and the bitter loneliness of neglect wraps these characters in an aura that sparks readers' yearning for justice and warms their hearts with compassion.

These five elements can be mixed and matched in any combination, though at least two or more are needed to generate empathy. None are more effective than others, though some are more appropriate to certain genres than others. For example, in a romance novel it's usually necessary that the hero and heroine be nice people. Likewise, a thriller wouldn't be too thrilling if the protagonist lacked courage. And in a mystery novel, it's pretty common for the sleuth to be skilled at, well, sleuthing. For example, Rex Stout's iconic detective Nero Wolfe is an expert at both crime and orchids, with a rapier-sharp wit, but he's nobody's victim and couldn't care less about being nice.

In romance novels, both the protagonist and the love interest need to be invested with empathetic elements, not only for the reader's sake, but to credibly motivate the Relationship Throughline. Good looks might initially grab the hero or heroine's attention (and tip off the reader to who the romantic lead is), but it's the emotional attraction of moral values and empathetic elements that compel them to be together and the reader to root for them as a couple.

Necessary Equipment

You don't need a necromancer or a really good friend-of-a-friend in the editorial department to learn an author's advice on a writing-related subject. All you need is their novel. Along with a pencil, a notepad, and a handy calculator. (Or, on the high-tech side, a stylus, a really cool note-taking app, and the mobile device of your choice.)

Oh yes, and a package of sticky notes. Post-It Page Markers work great for this, but a square pad of colored sticky notes can be economically cut into half-inch strips and serve the same purpose. A single color is fine, but two colors are better. You can get really fancy and add more colors later, if you desire.

Quick Five-Point Story X-Ray

A quick and simple way to get a broad perspective of any novel's working parts is to isolate five key points of the story. These five turning points represent the highlights of the protagonist's journey. They are where his internal and external worlds collide, and the truth of his character is revealed most dramatically.

A more detailed and comprehensive method of analyzing novels is detailed a little later in this book, but the basic tools and principles are the same.

The five points to look for are—

1. **"Problem."** The culminating event at the end of the first sequence. The main characters have already been introduced, but this event narrows the central conflict down to the protagonist and antagonist. The antagonist challenges the protagonist's flaw or fear, and the protagonist tries to hold fast. Whoever shows up here are the characters who will drive the story forward and define what it's about.

2. **"Commitment."** The culminating event at the end of the second sequence. The protagonist's goal is clear and tangible. He knows what he wants and so does the reader. Now he puts a plan into action that locks him into the conflict with the antagonist.

3. **"Midpoint Reversal."** The culminating event ("Cut Off") at the end of the fourth sequence and the initiating event ("Reversal") at the beginning of the fifth sequence, combined here as "Midpoint Reversal" for simplicity. This one-two punch by the antagonist gives the protagonist (and reader) a glimpse of how things might turn out, and strengthens his motivation to change.

4. **"New Direction."** The initiating event at the beginning of the seventh sequence. It contrasts with the "Commitment" event, demonstrating his character growth. The protagonist's old plan has failed, and he puts a new plan into action, based on the lesson he's learned. He does something he would not have been capable of before.

5. **"Sacrifice."** The initiating event at the beginning of the eighth sequence. The protagonist conflicts with the antagonist over the stakes, and the protagonist instinctively sacrifices the last thing holding him back from success. This is where the protagonist earns his satisfying ending. It contrasts with the "Problem" event.

These events occur at certain places in a story, and are easily located with the help of a pencil, note pad, and calculator. First, select the novel of your choice for the quick Five-Point Story X-ray. Choose one you've read before, are reasonably familiar with, and will enjoy revisiting. It can be as thick as Margaret Mitchell's *Gone With the Wind* or as skinny as Charles Dickens' *A Christmas Carol*. It doesn't make a difference because the locations of the five points are proportional to the novel's length. The example used below is from J.R.R. Tolkien's *The Hobbit*.

Next, open the novel, skip past the front matter (title, copyright, dedication, etc.). If the story starts other than on "page 1", jot down how many pages take up front matter and the page number where the story actually starts. If there's a Prologue, most of the time the story starts there. (For more about exceptions concerning prologues and epilogues, please refer to the chapter on "In-Depth Story Analysis.") Then flip to the end and note the page number where the story stops. *If front matter is counted in the page numbers,* subtract the first number from the last number to find out how many pages of actual story are in the book.

EXAMPLE

Front matter: 4 pages

Story starts: page 5

Story ends: page 306

Total story pages: 302

306	ending page #
- 4	pages before story starts
= 302	total pages of story

The Total Story Pages is the number that will serve as the foundation for all the following calculations. So highlight or underline or circle it for easy reference.

In the "The Leg Bone Connected To..." chapter detailing story structure, specific percentages are associated with each sequence and event.

These percentages mark the beginning and end of each event and sequence. For example, the first sequence "Upset Coming" spans the first 12.5% of the story. Its culminating event is nested within the last 2.5% of that sequence, so the "Problem" will be found at the 10% - 12.5% point.

Here are the percentage locations for the Quick Five-Point Story X-Ray:

1. Problem — 10% - 12.5%
2. Commitment — 22.5% - 25%
3. Midpoint Reversal — 47.5% - 52.5%
4. New Direction — 75% - 77.5%
5. Sacrifice — 87.5% - 90%

Now multiply the Total Story Pages by each percentage to identify the location of the five structure points. For example, 10% of 302 story pages equals page thirty. 12.5% of 302 story pages equals page thirty-eight. So the "Problem" in *The Hobbit* occurs somewhere between page 30 and page 38.

> EXAMPLE
> 302 (Total Story Pages) x 10% (beginning of event) = page 30
> 302 (Total Story Pages) x 12.5% (end of event) = page 38
> The Problem – pages 30 – 38

Repeat this process for each of the remaining story points.

> EXAMPLE
> *The Hobbit*
> 1. Problem – pages 30 – 38

2. Commitment – pages 68 – 75

3. Midpoint Reversal – pages 143 – 158

4. New Direction – pages 226 – 234

5. Sacrifice – pages 264 – 272

Remember jotting down the story's starting page after all the title, copyright, and dedication pages? Some books start the story on "page 1," but many count some of the front matter and start the story on a different page number, such as 3 or 7. When that happens an offset occurs that needs to be adjusted for in calculating the final page numbers for each structure point. For example, the thirtieth page of *story* in *The Hobbit* is not going to appear as the thirtieth page in the *book*. The four pages of front matter has pushed it to page thirty four.

If the story starts on any other page number than one, add the number of front matter pages now to each page number on the Five-Point list. This will adjust for the offset created by the front matter, and guarantee the structure points are aligned correctly with the actual page numbers.

EXAMPLE

The Hobbit

(Four page offset added to each number)

1. Problem – pages 34 – 42

2. Commitment – pages 72 – 79

3. Midpoint Reversal – pages 147 – 162

4. New Direction – pages 230 – 238

5. Sacrifice – pages 268 – 276

> 37.75   story's page #
> + 4   front matter
> = 41.75 book's page #

Now is the time to begin reading. If the novel is already familiar to you, it's often beneficial for analysis purposes to isolate the five points for comparison and contrast. So skip directly to the pages dealing with the Problem event. Read only that section and then pause to consider and take notes. Some helpful questions to focus on include: Who is the protagonist? Who is the antagonist? What is the big problem? How is the protagonist's flaw challenged?

When you feel satisfied that your notes have captured the essence of the first structure point, move ahead to the second. Read only pages containing the Commitment event, then pause again for notes. What goal does the protagonist want to accomplish? What's his plan to get there? How does his plan lock him into conflict with the antagonist?

Next up is the Midpoint Reversal. This is actually two separate events combined here for simplicity. Look for the cause-and-effect dynamic that draws a dividing line down the center of the story. How are roles reversed due to this event? Is the protagonist's glimpse of the future true or false, and who delivers it? What values are placed in direct conflict as a result (example: romantic love versus professional ambition)?

The break into Act Three occurs with the protagonist adopting a New Direction. This event sets his course for the final quarter of the story. What lesson has he learned during the story? How is it reflected in the new plan and purpose he puts into action here? How will the stakes character suffer if he fails?

The final point to consider is the moment of Sacrifice. This event unlocks and launches the resolution of the whole story. How has the conflict developed since the Problem event when the antagonist first challenged the protagonist's flaw? What does the protagonist let go of now that he would have never given up before?

Now that you've finished reading, sit back and take a broad view of your notes. Compare the Problem with the Sacrifice, and the Commitment with the New Direction. These two pairs of events mirror each other. The Problem and the Sacrifice are both essentially about the protagonist and antagonist in conflict over the former's flaw. The Commitment and the New Direction are both about the protagonist's plans to overcome that conflict. Contrasting elements of plot, conflict, and character between them is an excellent way to assess escalating tension and development of character growth.

I find it helpful to write down my observations on square sticky notes and paste them on a single sheet of printer paper, similar to the image below. By staggering the squares in a pyramid shape with the Midpoint Reversal at the apex of the triangle, it reminds me how the structural points build and reflect each other. (A printable version of this chart is available for download FREE at the following website: marymercer.weebly.com.)

Quick Five-Point Story X-Ray

PROTAGONIST: _____

ANTAGONIST: _____

Act Two
Act One

Problem (10%-12.5%)

Antagonist challenges protagonist's flaw, forcing him to make decision.

Commitment (22.5%-25%)

Protagonist launches plan to win goal.

Midpoint (47.5%-52.5%)

Role Reversal: _____

Antagonist cuts off protagonist's plan. Glimpse of future puts values in conflict.

Act Two
Act Three

New Direction (75%-77.5%)

Old plan failed, so protagonist comes up with new plan.

Act One   Act Three

Sacrifice (87.5%-90%)

Antagonist and protagonist clash over stakes, and protagonist gives up flaw forever.

Five-Point Example: The Hobbit

THE HOBBIT

Author: J.R.R. Tolkien

Starting page #: 5
Ending page #: 306
Total story pages: 302

Protagonist — Bilbo
Antagonist — Thorin
Mentor — Gandalf

PROBLEM / 10% – 12.5% / pages 34 – 42

PLOT: Bilbo hastily joins Thorin's company of treasure-hunting dwarves, and is sent on his first "burgling" mission into a troll camp.

CONFLICT: He's promptly caught, interrogated, and nearly eaten by the quarrelsome trolls.

CHARACTER: Bilbo is woefully unprepared for the journey's hardships and inexperienced in burgling anything.

COMMITMENT / 22.5% – 25% / pages 72 – 79

PLOT: Left behind in the goblin tunnels deep under the mountain, Bilbo strikes out alone in desperate search of a way out.

CONFLICT: He stumbles into an underground cavern where he's compelled to match wits for high stakes against the murderous creature Gollum.

CHARACTER: Timid Bilbo is so frightened by the prospect of being eaten, he can hardly think straight.

MIDPOINT REVERSAL / 47.5% – 52.5% / pages 147 – 162

PLOT: Starving in Mirkwood, the dwarves send Bilbo on a scouting mission into the tree tops.

CONFLICT: Unaware they are close to the forest's edge, he returns to report endless trees in all directions. (False glimpse.) "Dinner dreams" (more false glimpses) send the dwarves crashing deep into the forest in search of food, until they become lost and separated.

CHARACTER: Bilbo's singlehanded escape from giant spiders makes a different person of him, "much fiercer and bolder in spite of an empty stomach."

ROLE REVERSAL: Thorin was the dwarves' chief before. Afterwards, they look up to Bilbo as their leader.

NEW DIRECTION / 75% – 77.5% / pages 230 – 238

PLOT: Bilbo urges the dwarves down into the mountain's tunnels in a "desperate plan" to evade a surprise attack by the dragon.

CONFLICT: Sealing them inside, Bilbo boldly leads the dwarves along the only way out through an underground cavern filled with treasure.

CHARACTER: Bilbo becomes "a burglar indeed" when he takes the renowned Arkenstone diamond for himself.

SACRIFICE / 87.5% – 90% / pages 268 – 276

PLOT: Thorin's stubborn greed spurs Bilbo to leave the dwarves' mountain stronghold and plan his own burgling mission into the besieging camp of elves and men.

CONFLICT: He's caught by elvish sentries and interrogated as a spy or traitor.

CHARACTER: Bilbo skillfully carries out his plan to sacrifice the Arkenstone as a bargaining tool to prevent war, embracing his identity as a burglar at last. "But I am an honest one, I hope, more or less."

1st AND 5th POINT PARALLELS: Both are burgling missions into "enemy" camps, but whereas Bilbo's thrust into the first one unprepared and naive, he plans and initiates the latter with skill and daring.

2nd AND 4th POINT PARALLELS: Both are escapes through tunnels into caverns where deadly creatures dwell. The first time, Bilbo stumbles into a cavern by accident, lost and alone. The next time, Bilbo boldly leads his friends to the dragon's familiar lair, fiercely prepared to take on the scaly foe singlehandedly.

In-Depth Story X-Ray

Now that you have an understanding of structure and what to look for, and practiced with the Quick Five-Point Story X-Ray, it's time to learn how to apply your knowledge more deeply to novels. Structure is timeless and universal. Aristotle didn't invent it. He discovered it. Its enduring resonance across ages and cultures guarantees that whether a writer is a "pre-plotter" or flies through the pages by intuition alone, if the story works then structure is present. It's there, beneath the surface, waiting to be discovered.

So, pull out the X-ray machine, and let's see what's there!

Some of the following instructions repeat essential steps previously described in the Quick Five-Point Story Analysis chapter. They are explained again here purely for ease of reference, to eliminate the need to flip backward through pages. Many new details are included that are necessary to in-depth analysis.

First, select a favorite novel, preferably one you've read before and that's in the same genre you're writing in. Gather your pencil, notepad, and calculator (or digital equivalents). (Soulver for Mac or Soulver for iOS by Acqualia is a great, easy-to-use, combination calculator/notepad app.) Cut the sticky notes into sixteen half-inch strips, and write down the name of each event and sequence lengthwise on a separate strip. One name per strip.

Write the title of the novel, author, and genre at the top of the paper.

Drop down a little, and jot down "Starting page #_____". This is the page number where the story actually begins. Often the title, dedication, and copyright pages take up front matter so the story may not begin until about page six. Jot down the "Ending page #:_____", as well. This is The End page, where the last line of the story is, before the author's biographical information or advertising begins. If the story begins on any number other than "page 1," use the calculator to subtract the front matter pages from the Ending Page number to find out how many pages of actual story are in the book, and write down this number, too.

> EXAMPLE
> Title: *The Hobbit*
> Author: J.R.R. Tolkien
> Genre: Fantasy
> Front matter: 4 pages
> Starting page #: 5
> Ending page #: 306
> Total story pages: 302

When analyzing an ebook on an electronic device, set the font size to what's comfortable to read *before* jotting down page numbers. Keep in mind that should this setting be changed at any time, the page numbers will change also and all your reference points will be lost. For this reason, you may wish to make an extra note about this setting on your notepad.

What about prologues and epilogues? Epilogues are usually part of the Do or Die sequence, because most are concerned with tying up loose ends concerning the protagonist and main characters. However, I have seen a few epilogues that jumped away from the main story to set up a minor character as the lead in a sequel. If the epilogue feels like it's part of a different story (different protagonist, goals, thematic conflict, etc.), then exclude it from your calculations.

Prologues generally come in three types, and it will make a difference to the math which type it is. The first, and probably most common, is a relevant event from the protagonist's past separated by some time from the rest of the story. Take, for example, a historical western romance novel about a silver queen with a secret past who falls in love with the sheriff. The prologue might be the scene where her gambler father lost her in a poker game to the highest bidder, and she tried to run away. When Chapter One starts, it's fifteen years later and she's a wealthy and respectable woman. The prologue hints at the possible wounds she still carries from her past, but leaves the reader in suspense as to what happened during the intervening time span. Prologues like this are counted as part of the Upset Coming sequence.

The second type of prologue is a scene in which another character other than the protagonist takes the lead, but which nevertheless has imminent bearing on the plot. If this type of prologue were used in the historical western romance example above, it might depict a villainous bandit preparing to rob the train carrying the heroine's latest silver shipment. This prologue sets up in the reader the expectation of dramatic confrontation, but because it's written in a different point-of-view than the rest of the book, it benefits from being separated as a prologue from the rest of the story. Still, it serves the structural purpose of contributing to the opening sequence.

The last type of prologue is a teaser scene lifted from a particularly dramatic point somewhere ahead in the story, and repurposed as a prologue for the sake of dramatic tension. It's often taken from the Cut Off event or the black moment at the end of Act 2. Sometimes it appears word-for-word, other times rewritten from a different point-of-view. Using the historical western romance example, this prologue might be a preview of the Midpoint ordeal where the heroine's ugly past rides back into town just in time to interrupt the first big love scene with the sheriff-hero. Some readers don't appreciate being manipulated this way into reading half the book or more just to find out what happens next, only to read the same scene over again, but occasionally, when handled exceptionally well, it can work. Nevertheless, it does not belong structurally in the Upset Coming sequence, and should be excluded from your calculations.

Now write the following percentage figures and their corresponding events/sequences down the left side of the notepad. For your convenience, try to space them evenly. These will become the subheads to your notes as you X-ray the novel, so give yourself room. Often a book X-ray will typically run about four pages, so plan for about 3 - 4 events/sequences per page. Using a pencil and notepad encourages focus on the major points in the story, rather than falling into the temptation of getting caught up in jotting down intricate irrelevancies. However, there is also great benefit to using a word processing program with unlimited pages available, because the purpose of this exercise is to turn on creative light bulbs. And when that happens, you need the freedom and space to capture those illuminating insights in words. Both low-tech and high-tech methods have their advantages, and it's worthwhile to experiment with both until you find which one suits you best.

1. Upset Coming (0% - 12.5%)
   Culminating Event: Problem (10% - 12.5%)
2. Stakes (12.5% - 25%)
   Culminating Event: Commitment (22.5% - 25%)
3. Locked in (25% - 37.5%)
   Culminating Event: Fear Made Real (35% - 37.5%)
4. Breakthrough (37.5% - 50%)
   Culminating Event: Cut Off (47.5% - 50%)
5. *Initiating Event: Reversal (50% - 52.5%)*
   Stripped Away (50% - 62.5%)
6. *Initiating Event: Hope Lost (62.5% - 65%)*
   Win or Lose (62.5% - 75%)
7. *Initiating Event: New Direction (75% - 77.5%)*
   Final Push (75% - 87.5%)
8. *Initiating Event: Sacrifice (87.5% - 90%)*
   Do or Die (87.5% - 100%)

Here's where the calculator comes in. Take the number you wrote down as Total Story Pages, and multiply it by 12.5%. For my *The Hobbit* example, that would mean 302 x 12.5% = 38. Now you know how long the first sequence is.

EXAMPLE
1. Upset Coming (0% - 12.5%) pages 1 – 38

Next, take the number you wrote down as Total Story Pages, and multiply it by 10%. Then write down the sum after the Problem event on the notepad. Events are contained within sequences, so for the first half of the novel the ending page number for each sequence is also their corresponding culminating events' ending number. In the latter half of the novel, where events kick off sequences instead of drawing them to a close, the beginning numbers are the same.

EXAMPLE
Culminating Event: Problem (10% - 12.5%) pages 30 – 38

Repeat this process for each of the events and sequences on your list. When completed, there may or may not be one more number to deal with. Some novels count informational front matter such as titles, copyright, dedication, etc., while others just start numbering pages with the first chapter. If the novel you're X-raying is among the latter, you can put away the calculator. Yay! But if all that other stuff makes the story start on any other than "page 1," then there's a little bit more number crunching to do. It means front matter is offsetting the real page numbers and can throw off your analysis. The page numbers written down beside the sequences and events must be adjusted to reflect the page numbers as they appear in the book.

For example, if your Total Story Pages are 302, ten percent of 302 equals thirty. But because the beginning page count for the story was delayed by informational front matter taking up four pages, those four pages need to be added back at this point to correct the artificial offset. So in my example the equation looks like this:

EXAMPLE
302 (Total Story Pages) x 10% (The Problem event's beginning percentage) = page 30 (story location of Problem event) + 4 (adjustment for non-story front matter) = page 34 (real book location of the Problem event).

Remember to always add the Front Matter offset number last, *after* all other calculations are completed. Round page numbers (not percentages) to nearest whole number. My completed example looks like this:

```
  302    total story pages
X  12.5% sequence location
=  37.75  story's page #
+  4      front matter
=  41.75  book's page #
```

1. Upset Coming (0% - 12.5%) pages 5 – 42
    Culminating Event: Problem (10% - 12.5%) pages 34 – 42
2. Stakes (12.5% - 25%) pages 42 – 80
    Culminating Event: Commitment (22.5% - 25%) pages 72 – 80
3. Locked in (25% - 37.5%) pages 80 – 117
    Culminating Event: Fear Made Real (35% - 37.5%) pages 110 – 117
4. Breakthrough (37.5% - 50%) pages 117 – 155
    Culminating Event: Cut Off (47.5% - 50%) pages 147 – 155
5. *Initiating Event: Reversal (50% - 52.5%) pages 155 – 163*
    Stripped Away (50% - 62.5%) pages 155 – 193
6. *Initiating Event: Hope Lost (62.5% - 65%) pages 193 – 200*
    Win or Lose (62.5% - 75%) pages 193 – 231
7. *Initiating Event: New Direction (75% - 77.5%) pages 231 – 238*
    Final Push (75% - 87.5%) pages 231 – 268
8. *Initiating Event: Sacrifice (87.5% - 90%) pages 268 – 276*
    Do or Die (87.5% - 100%) pages 268 – 306

Calculating the decimal on percentage figures may appear obsessive, but when multiplying it can make a significant difference on all but the shortest novella length books. That half a percent in a really fat novel could ultimately mean the difference of eight or ten or more pages in the wrong direction. So calculating the decimal now at this stage saves a lot of potential confusion and unnecessary searching later.

When you know where the events and sequences occur in the book, place the sticky notes with the appropriate labels on their corresponding pages. Use one color for events, the other for sequences. If you are using more than two colors, use a third for the Midpoint events, a fourth for the Commitment and New Direction events, and a fifth for the Fear Made Real and Hope Lost events.

I used to stick them out to the side, so I could quickly thumb to a particular location, similar to using tabs in a Bible or dictionary. But I found they got in the way of my hands holding the book while reading. So now I place them sticking out over the top of the page, near the edge in a margin area where they won't block any text or get in the way of my hands. Whatever way works that's convenient.

Obviously, if you're using an electronic reading device, sticky notes will not be an option. Many ebook apps allow users to make highlights, bookmark passages, and insert notes. Anything that allows you to type in the name of the event/sequence *and find it later* will work. Searchable features are a genuine plus in this case. But if your particular app of choice is stripped of these features, it's okay. Colored tabs or fancy labels are a fun and quick reference aid, but not absolutely essential.

Will every novel hit the percentage marks precisely? Not very likely. (Though it's really cool when they do!) But the percentage marks are the "sweet spots" for where to look for each event/sequence. And generally a novel flows more smoothly the closer each event/sequence aligns with the percentage mark. The Problem can occur anywhere in the first half of Act One, but usually if it comes much later the reader may develop symptoms of impatience or boredom. Too soon, and important characters may lack sufficient setup for their impact on the story to be properly appreciated. Likewise, the Commitment event signals the beginning of Act 2, where the real meat of the story is. It's where the detective starts investigating the crime. The romantic couple begin exploring a relationship. The military hero accepts the dangerous mission. So it makes sense that while it requires some setup it's best the

Commitment occur at the 22.5 – 25% mark rather than later at, say, the 37.5% mark.

Why these exact percentages, and where do they come from? Who decided the Midpoint events had to happen around 50%? Or that Sacrifice occurred within the last half of the final act?

These percentages represent a consensus drawn from many theories of story structure. In my experience as a judge of award-winning published novels as well as a fiction writer and avid reader, they most closely depict the pacing of plot, conflict, and character development conducive to reader satisfaction. However, the X-ray process we're beginning is about recognizing and exploring patterns, both those successful and those less so. It is entirely possible and even probable to find a novel that played very loosely with structure in one part of the novel, yet adhered to it in others. For example, I remember a novel that had no discernible event breaking into Act 2 (which left me very confused about where the story was headed, because the protagonist had no purpose or plan). However, the ending soared to brilliant heights with a spot-on Act 3 that saved the book for me as a reader. While few novels are technically perfect, many novels have something valuable to learn from. Even if it's only cautionary ("don't let this happen to you") advice.

As structure patterns are recognized and explored, you will find that certain writers have their own structure they consistently follow. Some may have a shorter Act 1 or Act 3 in every book. Some may nudge the Midpoint events up a bit, so that the Stripped Away sequence is well underway by the middle. (This shows up more frequently when the Midpoint events are a "false victory".) When you find one of these writers and have X-rayed two or three or more of their novels, consider how effective their structural choices feel to you as a reader. Ask yourself, do you feel satisfied about how the story progressed at those particular points? Did your attention drift a little in places, did you start looking ahead for the "interesting parts"? If the author's structural choices worked for you, satisfying you as a reader, what compromises were made in other parts of the story to pull it off? Pay close attention to the level of your emotional engagement as you read, because it's your truest guide to whether the story structure is successful or not.

X-Raying a Novel

By now your book of choice probably looks like it's sprouted rainbow-colored hair, with sticky notes protruding high or low. It's time to put the calculator away, and get cosy in your favorite reading chair. The book X-ray is about to begin!

This is a book you've read before and enjoyed. That experience is valuable to this process. Reflect briefly on which parts of the story stand out most vividly in your memory. Did the opening capture your interest right off the bat? Was there a particular scene in the middle that still makes you smile or sigh? Did the ending make your heart clench? Estimate where these magical places might coincide with a specific event or sequence, and pencil a little star next to the name on your X-ray sheet. These are places you'll probably want to pay extra attention to, and which will more than likely inspire the most notes.

It's usually helpful to refresh yourself on the specific function of each event or sequence immediately prior to reading that section in the novel. I find it helps me focus on what to look for. You may want to take a moment now to go back and re-read the description of the Upset Coming sequence. Remember, the purpose of a book X-ray is to look past the luscious descriptive passages and scintillating dialogue (the fancy clothes and makeup) to see the structure beneath (the bones and joints) that make the story move and work on an emotional level.

As you read the beginning of the novel up to the Problem event, make notes on your X-ray sheet detailing how the writer uniquely fulfilled the purpose of the Upset Coming sequence. How is the protagonist's world already in trouble? Does he know it, but thinks it's only temporary or manageable, or is he in total denial? How is his flaw introduced in a way that preserves reader empathy? How is his strength demonstrated? Which main characters are introduced? How is the antagonist introduced? Which side do the characters argue for the moral premise, vice or virtue?

These are just some sample questions to inspire your creativity. I find that open-ended questions are more rewarding than checklists that can be answered by "Yes" or "No."

While each event or sequence will generate specific questions to consider while reading, some general questions are rewarding to keep in mind while filling out the X-ray. Try to identify which character is making the crucial decisions at each major turning point. (Tip: usually it's the protagonist, but sometimes the antagonist steps forward to provoke a response.) Follow the four throughlines, noting dominance and frequency of appearance on the page. (Tip: whichever throughline takes top spot at the turning points contributes to defining the story's genre, regardless of marketing. External Throughlines dominate mystery and thriller novels. Relationship Throughlines dominate romance and women's fiction. Internal Throughlines dominate literary fiction.) What does the character do at the end that he could not or would not have done at the beginning? Which character makes the big sacrifice at the end that enables the resolution? (Tip: it's usually the protagonist, but if not, it may indicate the story was really about someone else.)

Here's an X-ray example of the Upset Coming sequence from J.R.R. Tolkien's *The Hobbit*. The basic plot, conflict, and character observations from the previous Quick Five-Point Analysis are present in the following examples, but because this is an in-depth X-ray of the story, additional elements have been included.

UPSET COMING / 0% - 12.5% / pages 5 – 42

PLOT: Gandalf the Wizard volunteers Bilbo's services as a burglar to Thorin and twelve other dwarves on a quest to recover stolen treasure from Smaug, the dragon.

CONFLICT: "Sorry!" Bilbo says politely. "I don't want any adventures, thank you."

CHARACTER: Bilbo is an Enneagram type Nine, complacent in his comfortable hobbit-hole existence. He values respectability too much to face his own yearnings for something interesting to happen. Adventures to him are scandalous, upsetting, uncomfortable things.

EMPATHY ELEMENTS: Bilbo is a nice person who suffers unfairly at the hands of his uninvited dinner guests.

SEQUENCE QUESTION: Will Bilbo join the dwarves on their adventure?

When you reach the Problem event, stop reading. Return to the description of structure earlier in "The Leg Bone Connected To..." chapter and refresh yourself on the function of the next event you're about to read. Consider what questions you want answered, and then continue reading until you reach the Stakes sequence, making more notes as you progress.

Here's an X-ray example of the Problem event from J.R.R. Tolkien's *The Hobbit*.

THE PROBLEM / 10% - 12.5% / pages 34 – 42

PLOT: Bilbo hastily joins Thorin's company of treasure-hunting dwarves, and is sent on his first "burgling" mission into a troll camp.

CONFLICT: He's promptly caught, interrogated, and nearly eaten by the quarrelsome trolls.

CHARACTER: Bilbo is woefully unprepared for the journey's hardships and inexperienced in burgling anything.

EVENT ANSWER: Yes, Bilbo sets out on the adventure, but he's totally unprepared.

Repeat this process with each succeeding sequence and event until you have finished the novel and your X-ray sheet is completed.

Congratulations! You now have an in-depth X-ray of a novel's plot, conflict, and character development down to the bone-deep level. All on a few handy sheets of notepad paper.

As you X-ray more novels, store your structure sheets in an easily accessible file system of your choice. These are the words of wisdom you've gleaned from authors who have gone before you, showing you the way. Whenever an issue arises in your own manuscript that leaves you scratching your head (or pulling out your hair!), reach for your collection of book X-rays and zero in on the area or areas in question. Do you need to recapture your inspiration now that you've hit page one hundred in your manuscript? (A common place for stories to succumb to SIDS — Sudden Inspiration Death Syndrome.) Your notes on the Commitment event might relight your creative flame. Concerned about a sagging middle? Revisit your notes on the twin Midpoint events, along with some possible side explorations into the Breakthrough and Stripped Away sequences. Is a character balking and acting uncooperative in a scene? Hold a conference meeting with your notes to examine

how other authors established motivation in Act One and how the protagonist's goal develops through the major turning points.

In-Depth Example: The Hobbit

Here is an example of a completed book X-ray. Obviously, it contains major SPOILERS, because it details specific elements of plot, conflict, and character from beginning to end. Therefore, I highly recommend that if you aren't familiar with the book, please give yourself the enjoyment of reading it first before studying the X-ray.

THE HOBBIT

Originally intended as a children's story, *The Hobbit* has captivated young and adult readers alike ever since its critically acclaimed release in 1937. Together with its sequel trilogy, *The Lord of the Rings*, these epic high fantasy stories cemented author J.R.R. Tolkien's place as the "father" of modern fantasy fiction.

Often heroes in this genre, while typically ordinary at the outset, are nevertheless forceful and dynamic personalities who quickly take charge of the story's direction. Not so Bilbo Baggins, whom Gandalf assures the dwarves at the beginning possesses hidden depths and abilities. So hidden, in fact, that Bilbo himself has no idea how he can possibly live up to his PR. An Enneagram type Nine, there is nothing forceful or dynamic about his character. It isn't even his quest! It's Thorin Oakenshield's, and Bilbo is just along for the ride. Bilbo gradually takes control of the story via decisions motivated not by treasure, but by his integrity and unshakable devotion to his friends. By designing the central protagonist around relationships rather than the quest itself, Tolkien achieved a reader-character bond that's withstood the test of time.

While the quest is strongly focused on recovering stolen treasure from the fearsome dragon, Smaug, he is not the chief antagonist in the story. Appearing near the break into Act Three, he occupies a scant total of twenty-two pages before dying at the hands of a newly introduced character unrelated to the quest. His demise clears away any distraction from the Sacrifice event, when Bilbo faces off against the story's real antagonist. Who is this personification of the theme's dark side? The character who drove the quest from the start — Bilbo's companion, Thorin Oakenshield.

Title: *The Hobbit*

Author: J.R.R. Tolkien

Genre: Fantasy

Thematic premise: Haughtiness and greed lead to death, but courage and wisdom lead to wealth and contentment.

Starting page #: 5
Ending page #: 306
Total story pages: 302

Protagonist — Bilbo
Antagonist — Thorin
Mentor — Gandalf

—SEQUENCE 1—

UPSET COMING / 0% - 12.5% / pages 5 – 42

PLOT: Gandalf the Wizard volunteers Bilbo's services as a burglar to Thorin and twelve other dwarves on a quest to recover stolen treasure from Smaug, the dragon.

CONFLICT: "Sorry!" Bilbo says politely. "I don't want any adventures, thank you."

CHARACTER: Bilbo is an Enneagram type Nine, complacent in his comfortable hobbit-hole existence. He values respectability too much to face his own yearnings for something interesting to happen. Adventures to him are scandalous, upsetting, uncomfortable things.

EMPATHY ELEMENTS: Bilbo is a nice person who suffers unfairly at the hands of his uninvited dinner guests.

SEQUENCE QUESTION: Will Bilbo join the dwarves on their adventure?

PROBLEM / 10% - 12.5% / pages 34 – 42

PLOT: Bilbo hastily joins Thorin's company of treasure-hunting dwarves, and is sent on his first "burgling" mission into a troll camp.

CONFLICT: He's promptly caught, interrogated, and nearly eaten by the quarrelsome trolls.

CHARACTER: Bilbo is woefully unprepared for the journey's hardships and inexperienced in burgling anything.

EVENT ANSWER: Yes, Bilbo sets out on the adventure, but he's totally unprepared.

—SEQUENCE 2—

STAKES / 12.5% - 25% / pages 42 – 80

PLOT: Bilbo and company are first captured by trolls and then by goblins. The only bright spot in the middle of all this is a stopover at the elf haven Rivendell, where Elrond advises and prepares them for the journey ahead.

CONFLICT: Besides the physical conflict with the trolls and goblins, the dwarves quickly come to view Bilbo as more of a liability than an asset.

CHARACTER: Though Bilbo is a willing rather than reluctant hero, he nurses his own doubts about leaving the comforts and security of home.

EMPATHY ELEMENTS: Bilbo's an expert at moving quietly through the woods, and he's frequently in jeopardy.

SEQUENCE QUESTION: Will Bilbo be useful to the dwarves on the adventure?

COMMITMENT / 22.5% - 25% / pages 72 – 80

PLOT: Left behind in the goblin tunnels deep under the mountain, Bilbo strikes out alone in desperate search of a way out.

CONFLICT: He stumbles into an underground cavern where he's compelled to match wits for high stakes against the murderous creature Gollum.

CHARACTER: Timid Bilbo is so frightened by the prospect of being eaten, he can hardly think straight.

EVENT ANSWER: No, he's not very useful, and furthermore the dwarves abandon him.

—SEQUENCE 3—

LOCKED IN / 25% - 37.5% / pages 80 – 117

PLOT: Bilbo escapes the goblins with the help of Gollum's magic ring and is reunited with his friends on the other side of the mountains, a metaphor for the "new world" of Act Two. But this new world is full of new enemies.

CONFLICT: Wolves chase Bilbo and his companions up into trees, where they are nearly roasted alive until eagles (new allies) arrive to rescue them.

CHARACTER: Bilbo enjoys the praise of his companions for his successful goblin exploit, something he would have felt ashamed of in his ordinary world of Act One.

EMPATHY ELEMENTS: Bilbo is smart, compassionate, and in great jeopardy.

SEQUENCE QUESTION: Will Bilbo be accepted as a useful member of Thorin's company?

FEAR MADE REAL / 35% - 37.5% / pages 110 – 117

PLOT: "So ended the adventures of the Misty Mountains." The eagles carry Bilbo, Gandalf, and the dwarves high to their eyrie overnight until arrangements are made to deliver them farther along on their journey.

CONFLICT: Gandalf announces he's leaving them in a day or two to attend business of his own. Bilbo and the dwarves weep with distress, uncertain how they'll survive without the wizard.

CHARACTER: Terrified of heights, Bilbo spends an anxious night in the eagles' care, "for fear lest he fall off that narrow place into the deep shadows on either side."

EVENT ANSWER: Yes, Bilbo's accepted as useful, but without Gandalf along what hope do they have of surviving the dangers ahead?

—SEQUENCE 4—

BREAKTHROUGH / 37.5% - 50% / pages 117 – 155

PLOT: Gandalf leaves them with many dire warnings upon the edge of Mirkwood forest, where "the most dangerous part of the journey" awaits along a narrow path fraught with hunger and misery.

CONFLICT: They are hunted by goblins and wolves thirsty for revenge.

CHARACTER: Before braving Mirkwood, Bilbo and company seek safety at the home of the bear-man Beorn. Bilbo's "unimpeachable reputation" gets him inside the door, but it's tales of his "audaciousness" that wins food and shelter from this new ally.

EMPATHY ELEMENTS: Bilbo exhibits initiative and skill with his keen eyesight.

SEQUENCE QUESTION: Can Bilbo and company find their way without Gandalf?

CUT OFF / 47.5% - 50% / pages 147 – 155

PLOT: Starving without food or drinkable water in Mirkwood forest, the dwarves send Bilbo on a reconnaissance mission into the tree tops.

CONFLICT: Unaware they are close to the forest's edge, he returns to report endless trees in all directions. (False glimpse.) "Dinner dreams" (more false glimpses) send the dwarves crashing deep into the forest in search of food, until they become lost and separated.

CHARACTER: Bilbo's despair over their hopeless situation is contagious, and turns the dwarves' against him. "What is the use of sending a hobbit!" As if it was his fault.

EVENT ANSWER: No, and furthermore Thorin's leadership gets them lost and nearly killed.

—SEQUENCE 5—

REVERSAL / 50% - 52.5% / page 155 – 163

PLOT: Giant spiders capture the dwarves and prepare to eat them.

CONFLICT: Bilbo deftly secures his own escape. Employing the ring and his sword in an aggressive decoy maneuver, he sets out to save his friends.

CHARACTER: Bilbo's singlehanded escape from giant spiders makes a different person of him, "much fiercer and bolder in spite of an empty stomach."

EVENT QUESTION: Can Bilbo save his friends from death and captivity?

ROLE REVERSAL: Until the Midpoint events, Thorin was the dwarves' chief. From now on, they look up to Bilbo as their leader.

STRIPPED AWAY / 50% - 62.5% / pages 155 – 193

PLOT: Bilbo rescues the dwarves and leads them in battle against the spiders. Still hungry and lost, the dwarves are again captured, this time by wood elves. Once again it is up to Bilbo to rescue them.

CONFLICT: Giant spiders and grumpy wood-elves. Though Bilbo doesn't want to be depended upon, he can't desert his friends. It is up to him to take the initiative and come up with a plan to rescue them.

CHARACTER: Christening his sword *Sting*, Bilbo begins "to feel there really was something of a bold adventurer about himself after all."

EMPATHY ELEMENTS: Bilbo is a courageous leader, charging into the face of danger for his friends.

SEQUENCE ANSWER: Yes, Bilbo's wits and bravery win their trust and deliverance, but they have no food or provisions, nothing more than the clothes on their backs.

—SEQUENCE 6—

HOPE LOST / 62.5% - 65% / pages 193 – 200

PLOT: After nearly drowning in their river escape from the elves, Bilbo and the dwarves enjoy a "false victory" as their arrival in Lake-town is hailed with songs of riches and good times ahead.

CONFLICT: External: men and elves begin planning to claim a share of the anticipated treasure for themselves. Internal: the threatening heights of the mountain and the thought of the dragon haunt Bilbo.

CHARACTER: Thorin defers to Bilbo's leadership: "In the meanwhile what next?" Bilbo takes charge: "I suggest Lake-town."

EVENT QUESTION: Can Bilbo lead the dwarves to the treasure?

WIN OR LOSE / 62.5% - 75% / pages 193 – 231

PLOT: Winter closes in while they search in vain for an entryway into the heart of the Lonely Mountain. "Then suddenly when their hopes were lowest..." they discover the door and send in Bilbo alone. Smaug awakens and attacks, but Bilbo has a plan which the dwarves eagerly agree to.

CONFLICT: Externally, it's with Smaug, but internally... "Going on from there was the bravest thing [Bilbo] ever did... He fought the real battle in the tunnel alone, before he ever saw the vast danger that lay in wait."

CHARACTER: "Already he was a very different hobbit from the one that had run out without a pocket-hankerchief from Bag-End long ago... Already they had come to respect little Bilbo. Now he had become the real leader in their adventure. He had begun to have ideas and plans of his own."

EMPATHY ELEMENTS: Bilbo is smart and courageous in the face of jeopardy.

SEQUENCE ANSWER: Yes, Bilbo leads them to the treasure, but he awakens the sleeping dragon to attack.

—SEQUENCE 7—

NEW DIRECTION / 75% - 77.5% / pages 231 – 238

PLOT: Bilbo urges the dwarves down into the mountain's tunnels in a "desperate plan" to evade a surprise attack by the dragon.

CONFLICT: Sealing them inside, Bilbo boldly leads the dwarves along the only way out through an underground cavern filled with treasure.

CHARACTER: Bilbo becomes "a burglar indeed" when he takes the renowned Arkenstone diamond for himself.

EVENT QUESTION: Can Bilbo save his friends from the greatest peril of all, their own greed?

FINAL PUSH / 75% - 87.5% / pages 231 – 268

PLOT: Smaug attacks Lake Town and is brought down by the bowman, Bard, in a devastating battle that leaves the town in ashes. Afterwards, men and wood-elves unite to march on Smaug's mountain and claim the treasure to rebuild their lives. But Thorin, bewitched by pride and greed, rejects any claim offered by Smaug's victims and prepares for a winter siege.

CONFLICT: Smaug versus the men of Lake Town. Thorin's greed versus the wisdom of Bard.

CHARACTER: Bilbo has developed from a reluctant follower into an encouraging leader who inspires those depending upon him.

EMPATHY ELEMENTS: Bilbo is courageous in the face of jeopardy, and resists the lust for riches that drives Thorin beyond good sense.

SEQUENCE ANSWER: No, Thorin's greed becomes an unquenchable obsession, and furthermore threatens to plunge them into war as the army of men and elves besiege the mountain fortress.

—SEQUENCE 8—

SACRIFICE / 87.5% - 90% / pages 268 – 276

PLOT: Thorin's stubborn greed spurs Bilbo to leave the dwarves' mountain stronghold and plan his own burgling mission into the besieging camp of elves and men.

CONFLICT: He's caught by elvish sentries and interrogated as a spy or traitor.

CHARACTER: Bilbo skillfully carries out his plan to sacrifice the Arkenstone as a bargaining tool to prevent war, embracing his identity as a burglar at last. "But I am an honest one, I hope, more or less."

EVENT QUESTION: Can Bilbo's sacrifice of riches, comfort, and respectability save his friends from their folly and avert war?

DO OR DIE / 87.5% - 100% / pages 268 – 306

PLOT: Bilbo reveals his burglary and treaty efforts to Thorin, and is violently expelled from their company. Battle and bloodshed threaten, but when goblins and wolves attack, new feuds are forgotten. Dwarves, men, and elves unite against their common age-old enemies. Though the battle is won, Thorin is slain.

CONFLICT: Bilbo doesn't actually fight in the battle. His main conflict is with Thorin, who with his last breath renews his friendship with Bilbo, declaring the hobbit to possess "some courage and some wisdom, blended in measure."

CHARACTER: The battle is "the most dreadful of all Bilbo's experiences, and the one which at the same time he hated most—which is to say it was the one he was the most proud of, and most fond of recalling long afterwards." Bilbo returns home with Gandalf, who tells him, "You are not the hobbit that you were." He's lost his respectable reputation, but he doesn't mind. He's content, and richer in both friends and treasure for his adventure.

EMPATHY ELEMENTS: Bilbo is honest, even to his own hurt, and in the face of intense jeopardy remains loyal to his friends.

SEQUENCE ANSWER: Yes!

Trilogies and Series

There are special cases, like J.R.R. Tolkien's *The Lord of the Rings* trilogy, where a single story line spans multiple novels. It can get even more complicated when, as in Tolkien's case, each of the series' novels is further divided into separate "books." (Not counting *The Hobbit* as a prequel, *The Lord of the Rings* is comprised of five smaller "books" published as three novels, plus numerous appendices.) Another example is Diana Gabaldon's *Outlander* series, with its spinoff novellas. And George R.R. Martin's *Game of Thrones* series, which also has novelettes, and as of this publication date remains unfinished. Does the X-ray sheet cover one "book", one novel, or the whole series?

The answer is each and all of the above. Because structure is about engaging a reader's emotions, it is macro and micro. Structure supports the smallest scene of the slimmest novella just as it provides movement to the longest multi-volume saga.

When analyzing series, it helps to distinguish the difference between story arcs and series arcs. A **story arc** is a complete story line from beginning to middle to end, spanning either one novel or several. *The Lord of the Rings* is probably the most famous example of a multi-book overarching story line. A **series arc** is a longer story line, also complete from beginning to middle to end, that extends like an umbrella over the story lines of standalone novels. C.S. Lewis's *The Chronicles of Narnia* is a good example.

Example of overarching story line for a trilogy:

> *The Lord of the Rings: the Fellowship of the Ring* - ACT ONE - Frodo and company form a fellowship to destroy the Ring, braving many hardships and attacks before reaching the borders of Mordor, where the Fellowship is broken by betrayal.
>
> *The Lord of the Rings: the Two Towers* - ACT TWO - Frodo and Sam form an uneasy alliance with the creature Gollum to lead them deeper into Mordor, while Aragorn leads a small party to rescue the kidnapped hobbits from Saruman's scheme to destroy the ally nation of Rohan.
>
> *The Lord of the Rings: the Return of the King* - ACT THREE - When Mordor's Black Gates spew forth war, Aragorn leads the defense of Gondor and all free people in a desperate bid to buy a rapidly weakening Frodo time to destroy the Ring in Mt. Doom.

Each of the above books is completely dependent upon the others to make sense of the story. None can be left out. No overarching series arc is present (barring *The Hobbit* as a distant prequel and Tolkien's *The Silmarillion*).

Example of a series arc spanning multiple standalone books:

> *The Magician's Nephew* - FIRST SEQUENCE - The origins of Narnia, introducing Aslan and the White Witch. The

standalone storyline is about 12-year-old Digory and his friend Polly who discover alternative worlds, dying and about to be born, after playing with his uncle's magic rings.

The Lion, the Witch and the Wardrobe - SECOND SEQUENCE - Introducing the Pevensie children: Peter, Susan, Edmund, and Lucy. Four war orphans step through Professor Digory's magic wardrobe into a world of perpetual winter and take sides in an epic conflict between Aslan and the White Witch.

The Horse and His Boy - THIRD SEQUENCE - Set during the Pevensies's reign described in the last chapter of *The Lion, the Witch and the Wardrobe*, and involving a plot to overthrow Narnia. The story line is about a talking horse who helps a slave boy escape bondage. They form a friendship with another runaway and her talking horse, and together set out to reach freedom in Narnia.

Prince Caspian - FOURTH AND FIFTH SEQUENCES - The Pevensie children's second journey to Narnia 1,000 years after the first, when Narnians have withdrawn from Aslan's influence. The story line concerns Prince Caspian's quest to wrest the throne from an evil usurper, his uncle King Mirax.

The Voyage of the Dawn Treader - SIXTH SEQUENCE - An exploration of Narnia's farthest shores, and the return of Lucy and Edmund. The storyline is about Caspian's voyage to find and return seven lost lords his evil uncle King Mirax exiled.

The Silver Chair - SEVENTH SEQUENCE - A kingdom threatened with decline. The story line follows two children summoned to Narnia by Aslan to recover Caspian's only son and heir, Prince Rilian, who has embarked on a dangerous quest to avenge his mother's murder.

The Last Battle - EIGHTH SEQUENCE - The last days of Narnia. The story line is about the return of two children to save Narnia from an impostor who would destroy everything they hold dear in an epic showdown between kingdoms.

Any of the above books can be enjoyed and make sense apart from the rest. Indeed, the *Narnia* books were not written or originally published in chronological order, since Lewis had not planned it as a series. But taken together, they enrich the reading experience with a larger series arc concerning the world of Narnia itself, from its beginning to its end.

For either multi-book series with an overarching storyline or standalone books that contribute to a strong series arc, it is often helpful to complete book X-rays of each novel *and* the complete series as a whole. For example, if the series is a trilogy, you will have a total of four X-ray sheets. This is because as published, each novel in the series must satisfy the reader, or else they won't return for the next book. Therefore each novel contains a complete structure. However, the entire series also must sustain the reader's interest, or else they'll begin to feel dissatisfied and maybe even cheated that they've spent time on a story that's going nowhere. So the larger series will also contain a complete structure that (when done well) will overlay atop the combined structures of the individual novels, infusing specific events and sequences with even greater significance and meaning.

If you are planning a multi-book series, then I encourage you to X-ray a published series you are familiar with and that's similar in some important respect to your own project. Though it will require a lot more math to complete a super-sized X-ray of the overarching series, the extra work will pay for itself soon enough.

If the series is unfinished, as in the case of *Game of Thrones,* then a super-sized X-ray of the complete series will necessarily be incomplete for some time. However, many authors provide estimates of how many books will eventually comprise the entire series, and general calculations can be based on such information.

Here are some general rules of thumb regarding the "big picture" structural breakdown of trilogies and series with strong overarching story lines or series arcs.

Trilogy

Book One = First Sequence / Second Sequence. (Act One)
Book Two = Third Sequence / Fourth Sequence / Fifth Sequence / Sixth Sequence. (Act Two; sequences are squeezed shorter.)
Book Three = Seventh Sequence / Eighth Sequence. (Act Three)

Four-Book Series

Book One = First Sequence / Second Sequence.
Book Two = Third Sequence / Fourth Sequence.
Book Three = Fifth Sequence / Sixth Sequence.
Book Four = Seventh Sequence / Eighth Sequence.

Five-Book Series

Book One = First Sequence / Second Sequence.

Book Two = Third Sequence (may begin with culminating event of Second Sequence).

Book Three = Fourth Sequence / Fifth Sequence.

Book Four = Sixth Sequence (may conclude with initiating event of Seventh Sequence).

Book Five = Seventh Sequence / Eighth Sequence.

Six-Book Series

Book One = First Sequence.

Book Two = Second Sequence / Third Sequence.

Book Three = Fourth Sequence (may begin with culminating event of Third Sequence).

Book Four = Fifth Sequence (may conclude with initiating event of Sixth Sequence).

Book Five = Sixth Sequence / Seventh Sequence.

Book Six = Eighth Sequence.

Seven-Book Series

Book One = First Sequence.

Book Two = Second Sequence

Book Three = Third Sequence (may include part of Fourth Sequence)

Book Four = Fourth Sequence / Fifth Sequence.

Book Five = Sixth Sequence (may include part of Fifth Sequence).

Book Six = Seventh Sequence.

Book Seven = Eighth Sequence.

Eight-Book Series

Book One = First Sequence.

Book Two = Second Sequence.

Book Three = Third Sequence.

Book Four = Fourth Sequence.

Book Five = Fifth Sequence.

Book Six = Sixth Sequence.

Book Seven = Seventh Sequence.

Book Eight = Eighth Sequence.

Strong overarching storylines or series arcs in series longer than eight books are uncommon. Usually such series with that many books have a recurring protagonist whose adventures represent standalone stories. Edgar Rice Burroughs' *Tarzan* and *Barsoom* series are examples, with a few overarching storylines spanning two books at a time. David Robbins' dystopian *Endworld* series contains nearly thirty books, plus the thirteen-volume interlacing companion series *Blade*, yet major overarching series arcs span no more than about eight books. Perhaps there is a psychological limit to a reader's longterm attention span, since it may take years for a protracted overarching storyline or series arc to reach a conclusion.

X-Raying Movies and TV

While movies and television are a very different medium from novels, they are still crafted around the same storytelling principles. The typical scripted network television episode runs approximately forty-one minutes. Episodes on premium television (without commercials) run a little longer, at about fifty-three minutes. In word count, that's roughly the equivalent of a ten- or thirteen thousand-word short story. An hour-and-fifty-minute movie is like watching a novella told in sound and pictures. Due to these space and time constraints, their stories are intensely focused on the essentials. Characterization is often sharp and quickly defined. Conflict, both internal and external, is drawn into the open like water from a well. Key turning points are carefully built and boldly executed. Consequently these stories are a valuable learning resource.

With a little tweaking, the Book X-ray method described earlier can be adapted successfully for any scripted television episode or full length movie. By now you're already familiar and experienced with figuring pages to prep your Book X-rays. There's math involved in X-raying a movie or TV episode, too, but instead of page count, it's based on time count. Approaching the following calculations with a bit of patience will reap huge rewards in knowledge and understanding of how stories work.

First of all, select the movie or television episode you want to study. It's helpful to know in advance whether it was originally written for television with advertising breaks, as this may affect the structure. If you're not sure, watch for telltale "fade to black" moments at semi-regular intervals, often immediately following a point of high drama in the story.

Whether you are viewing a DVD, Blu-ray, or streaming the movie/ TV episode online, familiarize yourself with the time counter on your media device. It will be a crucial asset in preparing your Story X-ray.

Next, prepare your new X-ray sheet with the same percentages and event/sequence headings as for a novel. X-rays for television episodes will probably fit comfortably onto a single page, but plan for three to four pages for the average-length movie.

Near the top of the page, write the following:

> Starting time:
> Ending time:
> Total story time:

These are the film equivalents of "Starting page" "Ending page" and "Total story pages." Movies and television have "front matter" and "ending matter" similar to novels, which must be accounted for in your mathematical calculations. These are the opening titles and ending credits. Television often compresses these to thirty seconds for opening titles and a minute at most for ending credits. Movies may take a more leisurely approach, especially with the rolling end credits, which makes the official "running length" of a movie virtually useless for X-ray purposes.

Television episodes often insert the opening titles after a teaser or at the end of the first sequence. Because these titles typically go by very fast and would require a little more math to work around, I often ignore them. The thirty seconds difference they make are not always worth the extra effort. But if they take up more than a minute of story time in a less than forty minute television episode, it may become necessary to address them on your X-ray sheet. I'll show you how a little later.

Movie titles are generally introduced in either one of two ways. The first is the easiest to deal with for X-ray purposes, as it requires no additional calculations. Here the titles overlay some activity of the characters on screen, with the story pretty much getting underway right off the bat. The second style requires figuring math around a gap in the story. Here the story commences for a scene or two, then temporarily stops or disappears from the screen for the opening titles to roll through before picking back up again.

For television episodes with opening titles of thirty seconds or less, or for movies with opening titles that do not stop or delay the story, write down zero on your X-ray sheet for the "Starting Time." Fast forward to the end of the movie or episode and write down the time that the last frame of story appears on screen prior to end credits.

EXAMPLE

Television:

Starting time: 0:00

Ending time: 0:41

Total story time: 0:41

Now you may be anticipating an approaching dilemma associated with these figures. How do you calculate percentages of time when the clock is based on sixty (sixty seconds = one minute; sixty minutes = one hour) but percentages are based on one hundred? Never fear. It's much easier than it seems, especially if you have the handy chart I'm about to share with you.

First, remember that every hour has sixty minutes, and every minute has sixty seconds. So a movie with a "Total Story Time" of one hour and thirty-four minutes equals ninety-four minutes. (60 + 34 = 94) Converting the hours into minutes at this stage makes the rest of the math much simpler.

> EXAMPLE
> *Movie:*
> Starting time: 0:00
> Ending time: 1:34 / 94min.
> Total story time: 1:34 / 94 min.

Because you will more than likely be doing your math on a calculator, it's necessary to convert hours and minutes into decimals, and vice versa.

.08 = 5 seconds or 5 minutes

.16 = 10 seconds or 10 minutes

.25 = 15 seconds or 15 minutes

.33 = 20 seconds or 20 minutes

.42 = 25 seconds or 25 minutes

.50 = 30 seconds or 30 minutes

.58 = 35 seconds or 35 minutes

.66 = 40 seconds or 40 minutes

.75 = 45 seconds or 45 minutes

.83 = 50 seconds or 50 minutes

.92 = 55 seconds or 55 minutes

1.00 = 60 seconds or 1 hour

Time - Decimal Conversion Chart

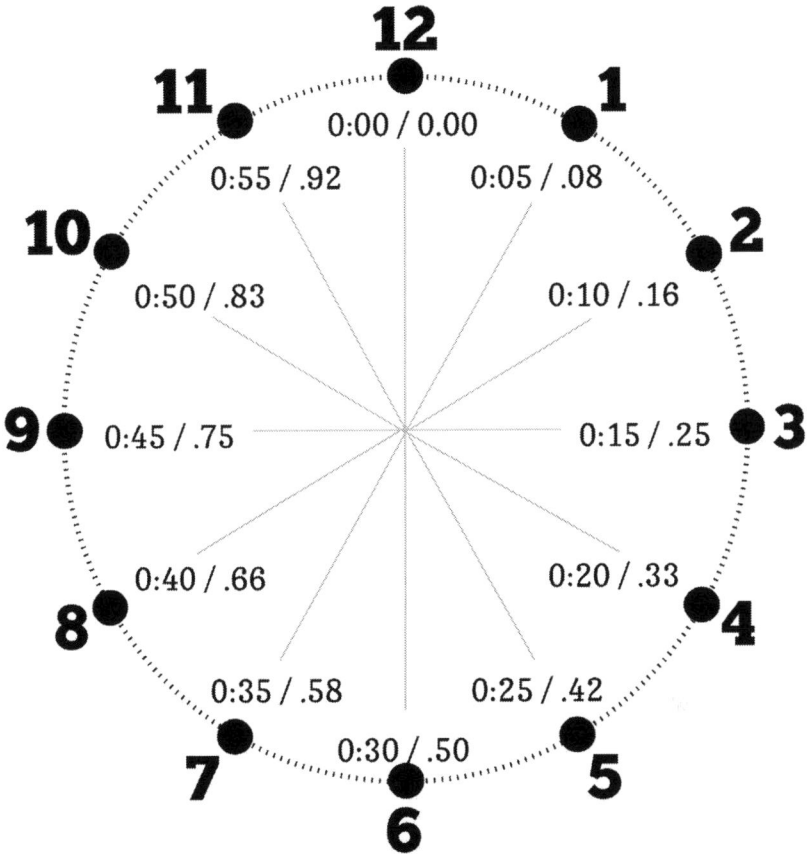

12
0:00 / 0.00

11
0:55 / .92

1
0:05 / .08

10
0:50 / .83

2
0:10 / .16

9
0:45 / .75

3
0:15 / .25

8
0:40 / .66

4
0:20 / .33

7
0:35 / .58

5
0:25 / .42

6
0:30 / .50

Now multiply the "Total story time" by the appropriate percentage numbers for each event and sequence labeled on your X-ray sheet. Refer to the chart above to quickly and easily convert the decimal figures on your calculator into clock time. Write down the answers.

For example, if I was crunching the numbers of a television show, my figures might run like this —

EXAMPLE

41 Total story minutes multiplied by 10% (Problem event) equals 4.1

My chart shows me that's about 4 minutes. Next I'll do the figures for the Stakes sequence like this: 41 Total Story minutes multiplied by 12.5% equals 5.125, which my chart tells me is close to 5 minutes.

The complete figures for a typical forty-one minute network television episode look like this:

EXAMPLE

0% - 12.5% / Upset Coming / 00:00 – 05:05
10% - 12.5 / Problem / 04:05 – 0:5:05
12.5% - 25% / Stakes / 05:05 – 10:15
22.5% - 25% / Commitment / 9:15 – 10:15
25% - 37.5% / Locked In / 10:15 - 15:20
35% - 37.5% / Fear Made Real / 14:20 – 15:20
37.5 - 50% / Breakthrough / 15:20 - 20:30
47.5% - 50% / Cut Off / 19:30 – 20:30
50% - 52.5% / Reversal / 20:30 – 21:30
50% - 62.5 / Stripped Away / 21:30 - 25:40
62.5% - 65.5% / Hope Lost / 25:40 – 26:40
62.5 - 75% / Win or Lose / 25:40 - 30:45
75% - 77.5% / New Direction / 30:45 – 31:45
75% - 87.5 / Final Push / 30:45 - 35:50
87.5% - 90% / Sacrifice / 35:50 - 36:50
87.5% - 100% / Do or Die - 35:50 - 41:00

But what if the opening titles *do* interrupt the story for a couple or more minutes? Adjustments must be made, or else the rest of the event/sequence positions will be falsely offset. Here's how to adjust your calculations around intrusive opening titles. I'll use a full length movie for the example, but the same method applies to television as well.

EXAMPLE

Starting time: 0:00

Ending time: 1:34 / 94 minutes

Total story time: 1:34 / 94 minutes

0% - 12.5% / Upset Coming / 0:00 - 0:11:45

Oops! Opening titles began at 0:07:10, lasting 2 minutes and 40 seconds. The story doesn't continue until 0:09:50. What happened to my Problem event at 0:11:45?

Because the opening titles don't progress the story, I have to figure out where the first sequence got extended to and where the Problem event moved after the opening titles shoved it out of position. Since they began seven minutes and ten seconds into the first sequence, that sequence still has another four minutes and thirty-five seconds remaining *after* the opening titles conclude. Which really means the opening titles artificially lengthened the first sequence. I simply add that time to my calculations for the Upset Coming sequence, then for the rest of the events/sequences I treat those two minutes and forty seconds like the informational front matter in a novel. Each subsequent event/sequence gets shifted ahead by that amount of time.

Continuing the example from above, I now have new numbers for my first sequence and the Problem event:

0% - 12.5% / Upset Coming / 0:00 - 0:14:60 (includes extra 2min. 40sec. opening titles)

10% - 12.5% / Problem / 0:12:05 — 0:14:60 (shifted ahead by 2 min. 40 sec.)

This may seem like more effort than a couple extra minutes are worth to figure out, but in film it's common for an entire scene to last no longer than a minute and a half. A three minute scene is long by some standards. So calculating the time taken up by opening titles can really pay off in the long run when identifying major turning point scenes.

Once the Story X-ray sheet is prepared with the percentages, event/ sequence labels, and time marks, you're all set! Butter some popcorn, grab the remote, and get ready to experience your favorite movie or TV show like never before — from the inside out. Analyzing films for plot, conflict, and character from a structural perspective is truly like traveling inside the story to its core. You get to experience every twist not only as a surprise, but as a purposeful progression in the plot. Clever dialogue exchanges burst with new life as you recognize thematic conflicts dueling for dominance. Quirky characterizations pulse with fresh insights into human nature.

Keep an eye on the time counter or set an egg timer to remind you when the first sequence is nearing conclusion and the Problem arrives. Pause or stop the film (if your player has the Resume function), and briefly note your observations on your Story X-ray sheet. A few sample questions to consider might be... Which characters were introduced, and how? Can you guess this early in the story what their Enneagram types might be? How was the genre conveyed by the tone of the initiating conflict?

When you've finished capturing your ideas, press Play again and watch for the Problem moment. Which character does it impact the strongest? What flaw or wound does it expose that must change or be healed by the end of the film? Stop/Pause and jot down your thoughts. Repeat this process through the remainder of the sequences and events until the final credits roll. Congratulations! You've added another inspired analysis to your personal treasure trove of story X-rays, which you can draw upon any time you desire for increased knowledge and understanding of how stories work.

One important note about television series. Each season contains a larger story structure, complete with episodes that serve key functions like Turning Points and the Midpoint. There'll be "catch your breath" episodes focusing on characterization and relationship building (Breakthrough; Final Push). Often the last one or two episodes of a season will have a higher degree of action and intensity, reflecting the final Do or Die sequence with it's initiating Sacrifice event. If there's a death of a major character or introduction of an important new character, it will probably occur at a key turning point episode in the season's structure, such as the Commitment event at the end of the second sequence, the Midpoint, the New Direction opening the seventh sequence, or the Sacrifice heralding the final sequence. Depending on how many episodes comprised the season (eight, thirteen, twenty-two, etc.), it's often rewarding to estimate where the season's Midpoint and Act breaks occur.

If you are unsure where a particular episode falls within the overall season, consult tv.com for detailed season information and episode guides. This website lists most series made in the United States and many other countries.

This same X-ray method can be used with scripts. A couple good online resources for movie and television scripts are simplyscripts.com and weeklyscript.com. Treat scripts like you were X-raying a short novel, but be mindful that even shooting scripts may read significantly different than the finished movie or episode. Film editors and other production professionals can have considerable creative input (sometimes notoriously so) even after filming is finished and "in the can." Additional dialogue or even alternate endings may be re-shot months later. It's even possible to re-cut scenes so as to completely switch genres; for example, what was written as comedy can be edited into drama. So even though a script may not be an exact textual representation of what's on the screen, it can provide a fascinating insight into the creative process and how a story metamorphosed into it's final form.

In-Depth Example: While You Were Sleeping

Here is an example of a completed movie X-ray. Obviously, it contains major SPOILERS, because it details specific elements of plot, conflict, and character from beginning to end. Therefore, I highly recommend that if you aren't familiar with the movie, please give yourself the enjoyment of viewing it first before studying the X-ray.

WHILE YOU WERE SLEEPING

A small-budget Christmas movie lacking any "big" names in the top roles and released in the warm months of the year, this romantic comedy seemed to have the odds stacked against it. Instead, its skillfully crafted feel-good story immediately captured the hearts of critics and moviegoers alike, propelling it to tremendous success at the box office and spawning international adaptations. The lead actress, Sandra Bullock, skyrocketed to instant name recognition and permanent stardom.

Deception is an integral component of pretty much all romantic comedies, since most protagonists in this genre must overcome self-deception on some level along the way to achieving the character growth necessary for a happy ending. The trick is the protagonist of a romantic comedy must not only be identifiable but also sufficiently likable that the audience buys into their being the object of desire and affection. Not an easy stunt to pull off when the character is lying to themselves and others. Which is where the brilliance of *While You Were Sleeping* pays off. The heroine is incredibly likable. She's a nice person, and though she feels invisible to the world, she has friends who recognize her value as a companion. (Even her landlord wishes he had her for a daughter-in-law!)

All this careful characterization of the heroine is skillfully balanced against the nature of the deception. First, Lucy doesn't start the lie. Her flaw triggers it (which is an essential part of her character arc and keeping her actively driving the plot forward), but it starts out as a well-intentioned misunderstanding. No one is deliberately trying to gain undue advantage over an innocent, traumatized family. Second, once the lie gets started, Lucy has altruistic reasons for continuing it (Grandma's heart condition; the family's general emotional state). Sure, her flawed goal benefits from it, too. That's part of her character arc. But the stakes she's concerned about aren't solely about her. Third, while the lie places her closer to her flawed goal, it simultaneously jeopardizes what she really needs to be happy, thus increasing viewer empathy.

―――――――

Title: *While You Were Sleeping* (1995)
Writers: Daniel G. Sullivan, Fredric LeBow
Genre: Romantic Comedy

Thematic premise: Living a lie leads to paralysis and loneliness, but taking honest action leads to love and happiness.

Starting time: 2:20
Ending time: 1:40:05
Total story time: 1:37:45

Protagonist — Lucy

Antagonist — Jack

Deflector — Saul

Mentor — Jerry

—SEQUENCE 1—

UPSET COMING / 0% - 12.5% / 2:20 – 14:35

PLOT: When the unsuspecting object of a tollbooth operator's romantic daydreams is mugged on Christmas Day and left lying unconscious on the tracks, she jumps in front of an express train and saves his life.
CONFLICT: External: the life-or-death hazard of the oncoming train. Internal: Lucy goes mute when her Dream Prince acknowledges her for the first time with a generic, "Hi, Merry Christmas."
CHARACTER: Lucy is an Enneagram type Four, filling her loneliness since her beloved father's death with romantic fantasies of a perfect love—fantasies that prevent her taking action that moves her life forward. She's timid and vulnerable, but she's also sensitive to others' emotions and experiences, able to reach out with genuine care and understanding.
EMPATHY ELEMENTS: Lucy has friends who like and rely on her. She's instinctively willing to place herself in physical jeopardy to help others.
SEQUENCE QUESTION: Will Lucy meet her Dream Prince?

PROBLEM / 10% - 12.5% / 12:05 – 14:35

PLOT: When her Dream Prince's boisterous family swarm the hospital room, a misunderstanding sparks Lucy's introduction as his fiancee. Learning she also saved his life, the stunned Callaghan family embrace her with open arms. "I always wanted Peter to find a nice girl. I'm so glad he found *you*!"

CONFLICT: The hospital won't give her information on Dream Prince's condition because she's not family.

CHARACTER: Lucy can't bring herself to correct the misunderstanding right away because of her concern for Grandma's delicate heart condition and the family's tearful emotional state.

EVENT ANSWER: Yes, but he's in a coma and her fantasy has trapped her in a lie.

—SEQUENCE 2—

STAKES / 12.5% - 25% / 14:35 – 26:45

PLOT: Peter's family encourage her to come celebrate a belated Christmas with them and meet Jack.

CONFLICT: Feeling herself getting sucked deeper into the lie, she appeals for advice to her boss, Jerry. He gives it to her straight. If she tells the truth, Granny dies.

CHARACTER: Lucy visits comatose Peter in the hospital, pouring out to his insensate ears her confusion, loneliness, and longing for someone to laugh and grow old with.

EMPATHY ELEMENTS: Lucy cares about Grandma and the family. She's also in jeopardy because a Callaghan family friend, Saul, overhears her nocturnal "confession" to Peter in the hospital.

SEQUENCE QUESTION: Will Lucy embrace the deception that she's Peter's fiancee and belongs in the family?

COMMITMENT / 22.5% - 25% / 24:20 – 26:45

PLOT: Faced with a TV dinner for Christmas and a disinterested cat for company, Lucy buckles and accepts the Callaghan's invitation.

CONFLICT: Saul intercepts her on the doorstep. He gently warns her he wouldn't let anyone hurt the Callaghans. "I wouldn't, either." Saul believes her.

CHARACTER: Lucy's longing for family compels her commitment to live out the lie.

EVENT ANSWER: Yes, but she risks exposure and widespread emotional pain.

—SEQUENCE 3—

LOCKED IN / 25% - 37.5% / 26:45 – 39:00

PLOT: Lucy experiences the "new world" of a Callaghan family Christmas, complete with her stocking hung on the mantel with care. Afterwards, Peter's brother, Jack, arrives while Lucy sleeps on the couch.

CONFLICT: Jack's instinctive reaction to news of the engagement: "That's not Peter's fiancee!" His suspicions mount when he catches her sneaking out of the house and later learns from her landlord's delinquent son that they're dating.

CHARACTER: Lucy loves this new world of belonging to a loving family, but is keenly aware it isn't truly hers and can all dissolve in an instant.

EMPATHY ELEMENTS: Lucy's concern for Peter's hungry cat. She's also the victim of injustice when she's unwittingly slandered by Joe Jr.

SEQUENCE QUESTION: Can Lucy pull off the deception without arousing suspicion?

FEAR MADE REAL / 35% - 37.5% / pages 36:35 – 39:00

PLOT: Convinced everything is not as it seems, Jack tracks Lucy down at Peter's apartment, where she's gone to feed the cat.

CONFLICT: Determined to protect his family's happiness, Jack hammers her with questions designed to trap her into a confession.

CHARACTER: Peter's sterile apartment embodies isolating self-absorption. It celebrates Lucy's greatest fear, which is a life apart from love and family, and reinforces the fact that her fantasy of Peter can never live up to what she really needs.

EVENT ANSWER: No, and furthermore Jack's digging for evidence to expose her.

—SEQUENCE 4—

BREAKTHROUGH / 37.5% - 50% / 39:00 – 51:10

PLOT: Lucy's accepted by everyone as Peter's fiancee and welcomed into the family with an engagement present which she helps Jack deliver to Peter's apartment.

CONFLICT: Confronted by Jack, Lucy proves her relationship with Peter by disclosing secret knowledge of his anatomy.

CHARACTER: Saul reveals he knows about the deception, but encourages Lucy to continue it because the family needs her. She didn't just save Peter's life. She saved the whole family!

EMPATHY ELEMENTS: She's in jeopardy of being exposed. She's encouraging of Jack's skill at building furniture, though he's reluctant to upset his father.

SEQUENCE QUESTION: Can she prove she belongs in the family as Peter's fiancee?

CUT OFF / 47.5% - 50% / pages 48:45 – 51:10

PLOT: Lucy and Jack get to know each other better. She reveals her dreams to visit Florence, Italy, and Jack reveals traits that let her glimpse her beloved father in him.

CONFLICT: The delivery truck gets blocked in for the night in front of Peter's apartment, compelling Jack to walk Lucy home.

CHARACTER: Lucy glimpses how satisfying and special a real relationship with a love interest can be.

EVENT ANSWER: Yes, but she's falling in love with the wrong brother.

—SEQUENCE 5—

REVERSAL / 50% - 52.5% / 51:10 – 53:40

PLOT: A very chaste and humorous "love scene" as Lucy and Jack literally fall into each other's arms.

CONFLICT: External: Crossing the slippery ice in front of Lucy's apartment. Internal: Falling in love with Jack creates conflict, because now her flawed goal of maintaining the fantasy engagement with Peter, instead of advancing her happiness, is an obstacle to her happiness.

CHARACTER: Spying Lucy and Jack together, Joe Jr. challenges her, "It's either me or him." Without hesitation, Lucy chooses. "Him!"

EVENT QUESTION: Will Lucy pursue her newly discovered feelings for Jack?

ROLE REVERSAL: Until the Midpoint events, Lucy thought her Dream Prince was the unattainable Peter. From now on she knows her Real Prince is Jack.

STRIPPED AWAY / 50% - 62.5% / 51:10 – 1:03:25

PLOT: Jack overhears a rumor Lucy's pregnant.

CONFLICT: He follows her to a New Year's Eve party where he unintentionally announces the pregnancy to all her friends.

CHARACTER: Lucy confesses her "affair" with Jack to Jerry at work, who advises her if she tells the family the truth she'll lose them.

EMPATHY ELEMENTS: Lucy has friends, and she's unjustly slandered again.

SEQUENCE ANSWER: No, and furthermore he seems to believe the worst of her.

—SEQUENCE 6—

HOPE LOST / 62.5% - 65% / 1:03:25 – 1:05:50

PLOT: Jack pressures Lucy about the foundation of her relationship with Peter, provoking a fight with her.

CONFLICT: Jack still isn't convinced she's Peter's type, or that his brother will make her anything but unhappy.

CHARACTER: Lucy admits to Jack her father wouldn't be happy knowing she's planning vacations she's not taking. Her fantasies about Peter are no longer sufficient to ward off loneliness. She doesn't have anybody.

EVENT QUESTION: Will Lucy come clean to the family about her relationship with Peter?

WIN OR LOSE / 62.5% - 75% / 1:03:25 – 1:15:40

PLOT: Peter awakens from his coma, and is diagnosed with partial amnesia when he can't remember Lucy.

CONFLICT: Lucy tries to tell the family the truth, but Saul deflects all her efforts.

CHARACTER: Lucy inspires Jack to come clean with his father about his own professional ambitions and take action to turn his carpentry skills into a business.

EMPATHY ELEMENTS: Lucy tries to do the right thing, and is in jeopardy of being exposed before she can pick the right time.

SEQUENCE ANSWER: No, and furthermore all her attempts are blocked.

—SEQUENCE 7—

NEW DIRECTION / 75% - 77.5% / 1:15:40 – 1:18:05

PLOT: Saul tells Peter how special Lucy is.

CONFLICT: Saul challenges Peter that he's a fool if he doesn't fall in love with Lucy and marry her.

CHARACTER: She's become so special to them, the family doesn't want to let Lucy go.

EVENT QUESTION: Will Lucy's fantasy engagement become the real thing?

FINAL PUSH / 75% - 87.5% / 1:15:40 – 1:27:50

PLOT: Confessing his duplicitous and self-absorbed faults to Jack, Peter decides Lucy can help him turn a new leaf and he proposes marriage.

CONFLICT: Peter's plastic-surgery-enhanced fiancee angrily confronts him over marrying "some bimbo."

CHARACTER: Lucy fires Saul and takes responsibility for telling the family the truth.

EMPATHY ELEMENTS: Lucy is a nice person who recognizes and values kindness in others. She's also unjustly slandered by Peter's real fiancee.

SEQUENCE ANSWER: Yes, but her Dream Prince is a complete fraud.

—SEQUENCE 8—

SACRIFICE / 87.5% - 90% / 1:27:50 – 1:30:15

PLOT: Jack gives Lucy a wedding present—a snow globe of Florence, Italy.

CONFLICT: Lucy asks Jack to give her any reason not to marry his brother. He replies, "I can't."

CHARACTER: Devastated by Jack's rejection, Lucy shoots out wedding invitations. She has Peter, but no matter how hard she argues to the contrary, she can't fool herself any longer. She's achieved her goal, but she's still alone and unhappy.

EVENT QUESTION: Will Lucy go through with the wedding to Peter, when she's really in love with Jack?

DO OR DIE / 87.5% - 100% / pages 1:27:50 – 1:40:05

PLOT: Lucy stops the wedding and sacrifices her flawed fantasy by confessing the truth, including her love for Jack and his family.

CONFLICT: Peter's real fiancee, along with her husband, crash the wedding, creating enough family chaos that Lucy escapes before Jack can catch up with her.

CHARACTER: Backed up by his family, Jack finds Lucy on her last day at work. She's moving on with her life. When he declares his love and proposes marriage, she accepts them all.

EMPATHY ELEMENTS: Lucy courageously faces her own fear of being alone, and is someone others care about.

SEQUENCE ANSWER: No, and furthermore not only does she get her Real Prince, Jack, but also a loving family and a real honeymoon in Florence, Italy.

Summary

Studying the work of other authors leverages reading pleasure into priceless insights into what makes stories work at a bone-deep level. "X-raying" a novel removes veils of personal bias and replaces them with the clear magnifying lens of genuine knowledge. You don't have to feel frustrated any longer when a novel fails to satisfy you. Or stymied when a book thrills you, and you don't know why. X-raying the novels you read empowers you to judge other writers' craft fairly, while refining your own understanding of story development.

The lifeblood of every great story is the characters. When writers find the pulse of consistent, realistic, empathetic personalities on a path to growth and change, either for the better or worse, stories come alive. Psychologists, self-help gurus, even talk shows have built entire industries around the human fascination with self-improvement. They tell people how to change, but there's nothing like a good story well told to *show* people what change looks like — both how hard it is, and how worth it.

Thematic conflict layers meat onto the bones of the story. It gives a novel meaning, resonating on a profound level of the reader's heart with universal truths about life. Regardless of whether a reader agrees or disagrees with the way the theme plays out in the characters' choices, the reader is engaged in the thematic argument. "No, don't do it!" or "Yes, that's what he should have done all along!" are exactly the kind of internal reader responses that guarantee an un-put-downable book.

Sequences and events form the bones and joints that provide a story with shape and twists, design and movement. They give the protagonist the opportunity to pursue a plan, and then the possibility to change course, internally and externally, in recognition of a higher purpose. This reflection of the human experience is one of the vital components of establishing reader engagement.

Successful stories are a blend of many elements working in harmony together to engage the hearts and minds of readers. A novel is more than a single story. It's several stories interwoven together. It's the story of the protagonist fighting against the odds in pursuit of a goal. It's the story of the protagonist fighting against his own flaws to be a better person. It's the story of the antagonist fighting against the protagonist, whom he believes is dead wrong. And it's the story of a relationship that means more to the protagonist than anything else in the world. These throughlines are the sinews holding the story skeleton together.

X-raying novels for plot, conflict, and character compiles an invaluable resource ready at your fingertips. It's a resource brimming with your own creative insights. It's a resource you can return to over and over again with the confidence that where other successful authors have blazed a trail down challenging paths of plot, conflict, and character—you, too, can follow and triumph.

Recommended Resources

— Plot & Conflict —

Deep Story: Hollywood's Secret Techniques for Writing Money Making Stories, by Carol Hughes. (Kindle edition; Carol A. Hughes; 2012)

The Inner Game of Screenwriting: 20 Winning Story Forms, by Sandy Frank. (Michael Wiese Productions; 2011)

The Moral Premise: Harnessing Virtue & Vice for Box Office Success, by Stanley D. Williams. (Michael Wiese Productions; 2006) Blog: moralpremise.blogspot.com

My Story Can Beat Up Your Story: Ten Way to Toughen Up Your Screenplay from Opening Hook to Knockout Punch, by Alan Schechter. (Michael Wiese Productions; 2011)

Myth and the Movies: Discovering the Myth Structure of 50 Unforgettable Films, by Stuart Voytilla. (Michael Wiese Productions; 1999)

Save the Cat! The Last Book on Screenwriting You'll Ever Need, by Blake Snyder (Michael Wiese Productions; 2005) Blog: www.blakesnyder.com. Community forum: savethecat.informe.com.

Save the Cat! Goes to the Movies: The Screenwriter's Guide to Every Story Ever Told, by Blake Snyder. (Michael Wiese Productions; 2007)

Save the Cat! Strikes Back: More Trouble for Screenwriters to Get into... and Out Of, by Blake Snyder. (Save the Cat! Press; 2009)

Screenplay: the Foundations of Screenwriting, by Sid Field. (Delta; Revised edition, 2005)

Screenwriting Tricks for Authors, by Alexandra Sokoloff. (Kindle edition) Blog: www.screenwritingtricks.com.

Writing Love: Screenwriting Tricks for Authors II, by Alexandra Sokoloff. (Kindle edition)

Techniques of the Selling Writer, by Dwight Swain. (University of Oklahoma Press; 1982)

The Virgin's Promise: Writing Stories of Feminine Creative, Spiritual and Sexual Awakening, by Kim Hudson. (Michael Wiese Productions; 2010)

The Writer's Journey: Mythic Structure for Writers, 3rd Edition, by Christopher Vogler (Michael Wiese Productions; 3rd Edition, 2007)

Writing the Romantic Comedy, by Billy Mernit. (Harper Perennial; 2001)

Writing Screenplays That Sell, New Twentieth Anniversary Edition: The Complete Guide to Turning Story Concepts into Movie and Television Deals, by Michael Hauge. (Collins Reference; Anniversary edition, 2011)

— Characterization —

Believable Characters: Creating with Enneagrams, by Laurie Schnebly. (Cider Press; 2008)

Deep Living: Transforming Your Relationship to Everything That Matters Through the Enneagram, by Roxanne Howe-Murphy, EdD (Enneagram Press; 2013).

Enneagram Explorations, Katherine Chernick Fauvre. Website: www.enneagram.net

The Enneagram Institute, Don Richard Riso and Ross Hudson. Website: www.enneagraminstitute.com

45 Master Characters, Revised Edition: Mythic Models for Creating Original Characters, by Victoria Lynn Schmidt. (Writer's Digest Books; 3rd Edition, 2012)

InsideOut Enneagram, by Wendy Appel (Palma Publishing; 2012)

The Literary Enneagram: Characters from the Inside Out, by Judith Searle. (The Editorial Department; 2001)

Personality Types: Using the Enneagram for Self-Discovery, Revised and Expanded by Don Richard Riso with Russ Hudson. (Mariner Books; 1996)

The Wisdom of the Enneagram: The Complete Guide to Psychological and Spiritual Growth for the Nine Personality Types, by Don Richard Riso with Russ Hudson. (Bantam; 11th edition; 1999)

Writing for Emotional Impact: Advanced Dramatic Techniques to Attract, Engage, and Fascinate the Reader from Beginning to End, by Karl Iglesias. (WingSpan Publishing; 2011)

— Script Resources —

Simply Scripts. Website: www.simplyscripts.com

Weekly Script. Website: www.weeklyscript.com

— Novels, Movies, & TV Used as Examples —

101 Dalmatians (1961)

A Christmas Carol, by Charles Dickens

Alias (2001-2006)

An Affair to Remember (1957)

Anne of Green Gables, by Lucy Maud Montgomery

Auntie Mame, by Patrick Dennis

Barsoom series, by Edgar Rice Burroughs

Batman Begins (2005)

Bet Me, by Jennifer Crusie

Blade series, by David Robbins

Bleak House, by Charles Dickens

Camille, by Alexandre Dumas

Casablanca (1942)

Comanche Moon, by David Thompson

Coming Home, by Lauren Brooks

Die Hard (1988)

Endword series, by David Robbins

Game of Thrones, by George R. R. Martin

Gone With the Wind, by Margaret Mitchell

Heartland (2007-present)

House (2004-2012)

Innocence, by Dean Koontz

Jericho (2006-2008)

Jessica's First Prayer, by Hesba Stretton

King Lear, by William Shakespeare

Laura, by Vera Caspary

Les Miserables, by Victor Hugo

Magnum, P.I. (1980-1988)

McLeod's Daughters (2001-2009)

Misery, by Stephen King

Monk (2002-2009)

My Fair Lady (1964)

Once Upon a Time (2011-present)

Outlander, by Diana Gabaldon

People Will Talk (1951)

Peter Pan, by J.M. Barrie

Prince Caspian, by C.S. Lewis

Rebecca, by Daphne du Maurier

Remington Steele (1982-1987)

Return of the King, by J.R.R. Tolkien

Rio Bravo (1959)

Robinson Crusoe by Daniel Dafoe

Romancing the Stone (1984)

Romeo and Juliet, by William Shakespeare

Sense and Sensibility, by Jane Austen

Smooth-Talking Stranger, by Lisa Kleypas

Tarzan of the Apes, by Edgar Rice Burroughs

The Adventures of Huckleberry Finn, by Mark Twain

The Adventures of Robin Hood (1938)

The Adventures of Tom Sawyer, by Mark Twain

The Alaskan, by James Oliver Curwood

The Beekeeper's Apprentice, by Laurie R. King

The Caine Mutiny, by Herman Wouk

The Fellowship of the Ring, by J.R.R. Tolkien

The Flaming Forest, by James Oliver Curwood

The Godfather, by Mario Puzo

The Grand Sophy, by Georgette Heyer

The Great Gatsby, by F. Scott Fitzgerald

The Hobbit, by J.R.R. Tolkien

The Horse and His Boy, by C.S. Lewis

The Hound of the Baskervilles, by Sir Arthur Conan Doyle

The Hunger Games, by Suzanne Collins

The Hunted Woman, by James Oliver Curwood

The Husband, by Dean Koontz

The Last Battle, by C.S. Lewis

The Lion, the Witch, and the Wardrobe, by C.S. Lewis

The Magician's Nephew, by C.S. Lewis

The Old Man and the Sea, by Ernest Hemingway

The Puppet Masters, by Robert A. Heinlein

The Silence of the Lambs, by Thomas Harris

The Silver Chair, by C.S. Lewis

The Six Shooter (1953-1954)

The Taming of the Shrew, by William Shakespeare

The Two Towers, by J.R.R. Tolkien

The Voyage of the Dawn Treader, by C.S. Lewis

The Wizard of Oz, by L. Frank Baum

To Kill a Mockingbird, by Harper Lee

Vanity Fair, by William Makepeace Thackeray

While You Were Sleeping (1995)

Wuthering Heights, by Emily Bronte

Appendix A

TITLE: *The Alaskan*

AUTHOR: James Oliver Curwood

1. Upset Coming (1st sequence) / 0%-12.5% / When Mary Standish elects coldly cynical pioneer Alan Holt as her escort aboard the *Nome*, her nearness jolts his stoicism. She's looking for a man to trust and believe in, but his love for Alaska and hatred of financial giant John Graham are his only passions.

Problem (1st sequence's culminating event) / 10%-12.5% / Alan becomes "involved in spite of himself" when he catches Mary in an apparent midnight tryst with Rossland, one of John Graham's agents.

2. Stakes (2nd sequence) / 12.5%-25% / Alan's cynical preconceptions about women are shattered as Mary gets under his skin, despite contradictory evidence she may be holding secret assignations with Rossland aboard ship.

Commitment (2nd sequence's culminating event) / 22.5%-25% / Mary secretly appeals to Alan to help her stage her own death... Or else she must really die. She cannot reach their destination alive. Deciding she's a liar or a fool, he refuses.

3. Locked In (3rd sequence) / 25%-37.5% / The next morning, Mary is reported gone overboard and presumed dead. Driven by responsibility for her death, Alan commences a desperate search and recovery mission.

Fear Made Real (3rd sequence's culminating event) / 35%-37.5% / Alan is forced to abandon the search for Mary's body, admitting at last that something stronger than guilt drove him. Despite the brevity of their acquaintance, he loved her.

4. Breakthrough (4th sequence) / 37.5%-50% / Alan travels alone across the vast Alaskan tundra, and in a fever-haze of grief hallucinates Mary is beside him and returns his love. Arriving home at his reindeer range, he finds her alive and awaiting him.

Cut Off (4th sequence's culminating event) / 47.5%-50% / With an honorable expression of sincere friendship and trust in him, Mary cuts off Alan's foolish dreams of love.

5. Reversal (5th sequence's initiating event) / 50%-52.5% / Alan slams back down to earth when he learns how Mary politely kidnapped gold miner Stampede Smith to guide her through hell and high water to Alan's home. She's a fugitive, but from what...or whom?

Stripped Away (5th sequence) / 50%-62.5% / Mary wins over Alan's men, so that when Stampede finds proof she's working as John Graham's agent, he almost doesn't tell Alan. Despite the seemingly incontrovertible evidence, Alan chooses to believe in her integrity.

6. Hope Lost (6th sequence's initiating event) / 62.5%-65% / Knowing Alan loves her, Mary offers to explain everything, warning him that the truth about her and John Graham is worse than any of his darkest suspicions.

Win or Lose (6th sequence) / 62.5%-75% / Mary is the runaway bride of John Graham, the man who viciously ruined and murdered Alan's father. Their love forbidden, Alan rides the range alone, planning to return stateside with her to confront their enemy together.

7. New Direction (7th sequence's initiating event) / 75%-77.5% / Far away on the tundra, Stampede delivers a life-and-death message from Mary urgently summoning Alan back home. Upon his return, he finds Mary trapped, Rossland occupying his cabin, and John Graham on the way.

Final Push (7th sequence) / 75%-87.5% / Rossland reveals Graham's plan to buy Alan's silence in exchange for isolation to rape, imprison, and murder Mary. Alan drives Rossland out, and the lovers prepare to flee to Nome.

8. Sacrifice (8th sequence's initiating event) / 87.5%-90% / John Graham's private army arrives and turns Alan's cabin into a deathtrap. Mary pleads with him to give her up to save himself, but he gladly accepts the loss of everything including life itself to protect her.

Do or Die (8th sequence) / 87.5%-100% / Alan sends Mary out through a secret trapdoor and remains behind as decoy for their enemies, sacrificing himself in a bid to buy her time to escape. She returns for him, and together they flee ahead of Graham's men into a ravine where Alan's shot and she's captured. Stampede arrives with Alan's men in time to dispatch Graham, and the lovers, now free, prepare to wed.

.

Appendix B

TITLE: *Jessica's First Prayer*

AUTHOR: Hesba Stretton

1. Upset Coming (1st sequence) / 0%-12.5% / An elderly, secretive opera-tor of a coffee-stall near the railway bridge has compassion on a starving and threadbare little girl, giving her food and a seat by the fire.

Problem (1st sequence's culminating event) / 10%-12.5% / Little Jessica wishes she could stay at the coffee-stall, where it's warm and pleasant. The cautious coffee-stall operator relents to allow her return the following week for a single meal, under strict conditions.

2. Stakes (2nd sequence) / 12.5%-25% / Jessica's contrite confession to stealing a penny smites Daniel's conscience, for he knows he is not a "very good man" as she insists and would have kept it himself. Wednesday break-fasts together become their routine.

Commitment (2nd sequence's culminating event) / 22.5%-25% / Jessica spots Daniel on the street, and surreptitiously follows him inside a church, which is like a fairyland to her. Much to his anxiety and dismay, someone now knows his secret double-life as a respected church-keeper.

3. Locked In (3rd sequence) / 25%-37.5% / Daniel drives Jessica out of the church before anyone sees, but her curiosity about prayer and God in-spire her to shrewdly find ways to sneak back inside every Sunday.

Fear Made Real (3rd sequence's culminating event) / 35%-37.5% / The minister's children discover Jessica hiding in the church.

4. Breakthrough (4th sequence) / 37.5%-50% / Scared Daniel will find out and she'll lose his friendship, but also driven to find out about God, Jessica allows the minister and his children to take her under their wing.

Cut Off (4th sequence's culminating event) / 47.5%-50% / To Daniel's intense anxiety and displeasure, the minister seats Jessica in front of the pulpit for Sunday service.

5. Reversal (5th sequence's initiating event) / 50%-52.5% / Jessica is intent on finding out answers about what a minister and God are.

Stripped Away (5th sequence) / 50%-62.5% / Jessica prays for God to repay Daniel for his kindness, but after extracting a vow of secrecy from her in order to protect his dual incomes, Daniel privately worries about how God will reckon with him for his avarice.

6. Hope Lost (6th sequence's initiating event) / 62.5%-65% / The minister visits Jessica where she lives in a miserable loft above a stable, but is unable to help her.

Win or Lose (6th sequence) / 62.5%-75% / Jessica keeps Daniel's secret from the minister, who provides the child with enough money for daily breakfasts at the coffee-stall.

7. New Direction (7th sequence's initiating event) / 75%-77.5% / Jessica fails to show up for Sunday services or for breakfast with Daniel two weeks in a row.

Final Push (7th sequence) / 75%-87.5% / Daniel's anxiety for Jessica overcomes his fear of discovery, and he risks enlisting the minister's assistance to locate the child. Finding her deathly ill, he repents for loving money more than people.

8. Sacrifice (8th sequence's initiating event) / 87.5%-90% / Daniel abandons the coffee-stall to nurse Jessica in his own home and sends a message summoning the minister to the dying child's bedside. His heart turns to God, and he repents of his sins.

Do or Die (8th sequence) / 87.5%-100% / Daniel would rather give away every penny he's earned than lose the child, and confesses his double life to the minister. Seeing how much she means to Daniel, Jessica prays and is restored to a healthy, happy life as his foster daughter.

Appendix C

TITLE: *Tarzan of the Apes*

AUTHOR: Edgar Rice Burroughs

1. Upset Coming (1st sequence) / 0%-12.5% / Newlyweds Lord Greystoke and Lady Alice, en route to a British diplomatic posting, are stranded by mutineers on the untamed coast of darkest Africa. Their struggle for survival against jungle and beasts is punctuated by the birth of their son and the death of Lady Alice.

Problem (1st sequence's culminating event) / 10%-12.5% / The great apes attack and kill Lord Greystoke, but his infant son is rescued and adopted by a female ape recently bereft of her own baby.

2. Stakes (2nd sequence) / 12.5%-25% / Tarzan grows up a hated misfit among his ape tribe, though loved by his ape mother. Discovering an abandoned cabin stocked with English-language books, he begins a journey of knowledge, and grows into a mighty killer.

Commitment (2nd sequence's culminating event) / 22.5%-25% / Tarzan kills his lifelong ape enemy in hand-to-hand combat, and desires to set himself apart as a man clothed.

3. Locked In (3rd sequence) / 25%-37.5% / Cannibals slay Tarzan's ape mother, and his vengeance leads him back to their camp. He discovers much practical knowledge from his first encounter with mankind, enabling him to become King of the Apes.

Fear Made Real (3rd sequence's culminating event) / 35%-37.5% / Tarzan defeats a challenger to his throne, Terkoz, but in the way of rational man lets him live. Renouncing the ways of the apes, he takes "his first step toward the goal which he had set," and leaves to find civilized men.

4. Breakthrough (4th sequence) / 37.5%-50% / A ship arrives on the coast of Africa, marooning a group of hapless adventurers on the beach. Tarzan watches from a distance and wonders at the strange newcomers, among whom is the beautiful American, Jane Porter.

Cut Off (4th sequence's culminating event) / 47.5%-50% / A lioness attacks Jane in Lord and Lady Greystoke's abandoned cabin. Tarzan attacks and kills the lioness with his bare hands, saving Jane's life, though she only catches a glimpse of him.

5. Reversal (5th sequence's initiating event) / 50%-52.5% / Tarzan stealthily rescues Jane's absentminded father and academic friend from a lion attack on the beach.

Stripped Away (5th sequence) / 50%-62.5% / Tarzan cautiously befriends helpless members of the marooned party, one of whom is a relative of the deceased Lord and Lady Greystoke, whose remains are discovered and given proper burial. Tarzan falls in love from afar with the cultured Jane.

6. Hope Lost (6th sequence's initiating event) / 62.5%-65% / Just as Tarzan prepares to declare his love for her, Jane is kidnapped by the exiled ape, Terkoz, who is bent on revenge. While her loved ones abandon all hope, Tarzan gives pursuit and rescues her.

Win or Lose (6th sequence) / 62.5%-75% / Sheltered by the jungle, Tarzan and Jane's innocent love flourishes until civilization closes in on them in the form of a French naval rescue party. When the French fall into the clutches of cannibals, Tarzan leaves Jane to rescue them.

7. New Direction (7th sequence's initiating event) / 75%-77.5% / The captured French are given up for dead. Jane's jealous suitor accuses her missing forest god of conspiring with the cannibals, unaware that Tarzan has taken a surviving officer into his care.

Final Push (7th sequence) / 75%-87.5% / Tarzan faithfully tends Lieutenant D'Arnot's severe wounds, though caring for his new friend delays his yearned for return to Jane. She waits, but is finally compelled to leave Africa—and her forest lover—behind.

8. Sacrifice (8th sequence's initiating event) / 87.5%-90% / Tarzan sacrifices his jungle life to search for Jane and return D'Arnot to civilization, where his soul chafes even as he becomes a fine gentleman.

Do or Die (8th sequence) / 87.5%-100% / Awaiting evidence that he's the son and true heir of Lord Greystoke, Tarzan locates Jane in time to save her from a forest fire, but too late to save her from choosing security over love. Brokenhearted, he denies his aristocratic birth and returns to the African jungle.

CRAFT AN EMOTIONALLY CHARGED STORY
THAT KEEPS READERS TURNING PAGES

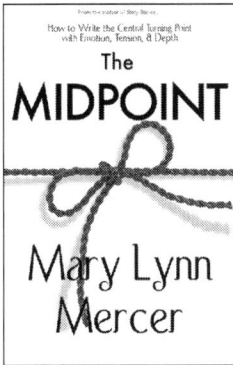

Have you ever started writing a story, feeling full of inspiration and enthusiasm, only to lose direction somewhere in the middle?

Grab hold of a bright lifeline for writers trekking across their novel's swampy middle. Like Ariadne's thread guiding Theseus through the treacherous labyrinth, there exists a scarlet cord to help successfully navigate from beginning to end.

Much more than a "plot point" to energize pacing, the Midpoint is the central nervous system controlling the entire story. Mastering the Midpoint helps writers survive and thrive in the Everglades of the middle. Rediscover the spark in your story by learning how to–

- Design a Midpoint with depth by crafting realistic, multi-dimensional character flaws that resonate emotionally with readers.

- Strategically position the Midpoint at the apex of a simple four-step story structure that reflects realistic human self-improvement.

- Connect the three key events (the Midpoint is one of them!) in every story that are absolutely vital to creating escalating tension.

- Translate the eight essential functions of the Midpoint into specific beats and scenes reflecting your unique creative vision.

- Apply three quick and easy "tools" to craft Midpoints with maximum dramatic impact.

Ignite your creativity while enjoying dozens of examples from novels, television, and movies. Fantasy, inspirational, mystery, science fiction, western, young adult, romantic suspense, and contemporary/historical romance–every genre contributes valuable insights.

Available now in ebook and print.

ISBN: 0-692-23862-X   ISBN-13: 978-0-692-23862-2

Printed in Great Britain
by Amazon